JOHN RICHARDSON w⸱⸱⸱ ⸱⸱⸱ ⸱⸱⸱ ⸱⸱⸱ in the
coffee-bar and restauran⸱⸱⸱ ⸱⸱⸱ ⸱⸱⸱ largest
sandwich business in Irel⸱⸱⸱ ⸱⸱⸱ *Wake
Up and Smell the Profit:* ⸱⸱⸱ *oney in
Your Coffee Business* and *⸱⸱⸱ ⸱⸱⸱ Setting
Up and Managing Your Own Coffee Bar.* He lives with his wife and
daughter in Bangor, Northern Ireland. A keen golfer, he is also the
author of the bestselling book *Dream On: One Hacker's Challenge to
Break Par in a Year* (Blackstaff Press, 2009).

50 GREATEST GOLF TIPS

JOHN RICHARDSON

·THE·
BLACK
·STAFF·
PRESS

First published in 2014 by
Blackstaff Press
4D Weavers Court, Linfield Road
Belfast, BT12 5GH

with the assistance of
The Arts Council of Northern Ireland

© John Richardson, 2014

Typeset by KT Designs, St Helens, England

Printed and bound by by CPI Group UK (Ltd), Croydon CR0 4YY

A CIP catalogue record for this book is available
from the British Library

ISBN 978 0 85640 926 4

www.blackstaffpress.com
www.breakparblueprint.com
www.fiftygreatgolftips.com

For every amateur golfer
still searching for the 'secret' …

CONTENTS

Video content

Golf instruction is tricky at the best of times but attempting to use just the written word can be the most confusing form of instruction of all.

To lessen this confusion we have created a video to accompany each tip and these can be found at:

www.fiftygreatgolftips.com

You'll also get to see a few of the tips that missed the cut as well as a broader explanation of the seven-step process for golf improvement.

Introduction

I'm not a professional golfer, I've never played in a Ryder Cup and sadly I haven't joined the ranks of those Northern Irish golfers who have bagged a major or two. What I am is an average amateur golfer who managed to make a very un-average improvement to my golf in a relatively short period of time. During that time I came pretty close to trying every golf tip out there and had varying levels of success. These days, after a relatively long career owning my own businesses, I operate as a business consultant to a very large range of enterprises.

So, as both a golfer and a business consultant, I'm obsessed with finding tips, techniques, strategies or ideas that actually work. Tips that the average golfer can use. Not a Rory, Darren, Graeme or Padraig, but a time-starved, cash-limited and possibly creaky-backed golfer like the rest of us.

A few years ago I embarked on a challenge that, for better or worse, was deemed impossible by the golfing community at every level. When asked about my chances, Ryder Cup legend Sam Torrance told me to 'dream on', and Darren Clarke suggested that three years was the shortest possible timeline for what I was attempting to do. When I ventured into the Wild West of the internet golf forums to post about my challenge I encountered everything from friendly scepticism to extreme and hilariously personal abuse.

The challenge was pretty simple. My aim was to change from being a golfer who couldn't break par to being one who could shoot a level par round or better within a year, while holding down a 50-hour-a-week job. I had a full 365 days to take my control round of 103 down to 71 or better. I decided to attempt this at the Blackwood Golf Centre, my local course in Bangor, County Down, in large part because it was a 6,300-yard, par 71 course, with an additional, and challenging, par 3 course and a high-quality driving range. I also had a good relationship with the managers of the centre, having previously managed the bar and catering facilities.

During that year I hit over 70,000 golf balls in practice, watched dozens of DVDs, YouTube posts and old videos, read over 60 books (and countless magazine articles) on golf improvement, and had some great, albeit brief, conversations with some truly great golfers. I picked up some exceptional tips and these had a substantial and quantifiable effect on my progress. To cut a very long story short, after some epic highs and multiple humiliating lows, I eventually managed, 362 days after I had started, to shoot a 70 at Blackwood – one under par.

The full story of my challenge can be found in my book *Dream On: One hacker's challenge to break par in a year*. Sam Torrance may have doubted my ability to shoot a par round but he certainly provided me with a great title for the book!

But perhaps of more interest to you is what I've done with my golf subsequently. Golf is a sport that gets under your skin so, since I finished the challenge, I have continued to study the ways that golfers improve. I set up a business called the Break Par Blueprint which has now worked with more than 3,000 golfers to help them produce tangible and rapid improvement.

I have also had the opportunity to speak to some of the best coaches and players in the world and whilst this has been a wonderful journey it has also made me realise just how confusing and conflicting golfing advice can be. Golfers, like the rest of mankind, are obsessed with immediate gratification and the promise of instant results. We have a tendency to believe that Ben Hogan really did find the 'secret' and barely a year passes without some new book purporting to have discovered it, whilst conveniently explaining that all previous discoveries were wrong.

This book is different in that it brings together the very best tips that I have discovered – tips that can help you to make real progress. It's about sorting the wheat from the chaff and showing what has really worked, not just for me, but also for the many golfers I have worked with, spoken to, played with and read about.

A word of caution – by their nature, in many cases

tips provide Band-Aids to problems that have developed over time rather than looking at your game as a whole and seeing how your scoring can be improved in a more holistic fashion. I'm aware how irritating that word is, but in this case I'm not talking about weird alternative therapies. I'm taking about looking at all the aspects of your golf game, considering the way they interact, and then coming up with a plan for improvement. In a very few cases, you may just need a few excellent tips or drills but very often what you think you need to improve is not what is necessary for long-term improvement.

The second thorny issue is that there will always be different opinions on what will fix different problems. I once played a round of golf with the editor of one of the largest golf magazines in the world and he talked about how most editions of the magazine contained conflicting advice from different coaches or players. Rather than attempting to persuade the contributors to alter their tips, they positioned them as far apart in the magazine as possible in the hope that readers wouldn't notice!

So the point really is that you should take the tips in this book, however good they may be, within the context of the fact that they can be occasionally conflicting and must ideally be part of a structured long-term golf improvement process.

The 1,000 hours/1 per cent rule

Ever since I completed my initial golf challenge in 2006 and through a lot of contact with coaching clients (outside of the golf arena) I've become convinced that you can fundamentally change your life in about 1,000 hours of really focused action. If you're prepared to give up television (we watch an average of about 27 hours a week in the UK and in the US that figure is higher) for a year, the world can become your oyster. You can, almost without exception, put yourself into the top 1 per cent of the field in which you're trying to succeed. And great things can happen in that top 1 per cent.

- It took me 1,000 hours of dedicated work to break par – and less than 1 per cent of golfers ever break par.

- It took me 1,000 hours of dedicated work (outside what I was doing during the day) to completely reinvent my first hospitality business and sell it for an income multiple hitherto unheard of for a business of that type. Less than 5 per cent of hospitality businesses last for more than ten years. Only a tiny fraction of that number become enterprises that are copied and modelled as examples of excellence.

- It took 1,000 hours of work to understand how to create books that resonate with different marketplaces. Eighty-six per cent of Americans want to write a book, less than 1 per cent actually do.

- It then took 1,000 hours to turn these books into bestsellers. Considerably less than 1 per cent of all books printed – probably more like less than 0.1 per cent – reach long-term bestseller status.

These are just four examples of the way in which I've applied this principle. At the heart of each of these projects have been two key concepts.

1. Each hour of that 1,000 has to be ruthlessly focused on improvement. One thousand hours of thrashing away at the range or playing your usual rounds will not make the difference. Each hour must count and must move you towards your end goal.

2. Each hour of that 1,000 has to be focused upon the creation of a multi-step process that can start to form an infrastructure under which you improve. The faster you move towards the understanding of a process for your improvement, the faster you'll reach your goal. Without a coherent process or formula for each project, you'll never become one of that magical 1 per cent.

So this book should sit within the context of an overall formula that can be used to make a long-term improvement.

I've highlighted the full formula we use in the blueprint below so that you can see how many of these tips fit with that broader context.

The process

The core process for improvement in golf is as follows:

1. **Fundamentals** – understand and work on a continual basis to ensure that the fundamentals of the set up and swing are correct.

2. **Fix** – ruthlessly attack any problems with structured drills.

3. **Short game** – focus on the short game as a cornerstone of scoring.

4. **Putting** – create a consistent, confident putting stroke.

5. **Long game** – master all aspects of the longer clubs to ensure the short game can be put in play.

6. **Course management** – dissect in detail the best way to get around the course.

7. **Mental game** – understand that once the fundamentals are sorted and the fix is in place, the game of golf is an almost entirely in your head.

The overriding principle that governs any improvement strategy

There are different ways of using this book: you may want to dip in and out and take a few tips that are especially relevant to your game, or you may want to use it to transform your game.

If you are intrigued by some of the underlying processes behind my golf challenge or simply feel that now is the right time to make a big improvement in your own game then the click process will be vital for you. This process, coupled with the underlying principles of the 1,000-hour challenge, is something that has now been tested with tens of thousands of employees in organisational environments. It also works for individuals who would like to make a substantial change in a specific area of their lives.

The process has three starting steps, and then four underlying rules which create a solid platform for seeing the challenge or change through to a satisfactory conclusion. The three steps are as follows:

1. Ensure that you have quantifiable and crystal-clear goals

Any programme of change, whether in golf, business, weight loss or any other field, must start with a crystal-clear goal which will give you a planned outcome which you can buy into. In my golf challenge, for example, I had 365 days in which to shoot a level or sub-par round. In weight loss the goal could be losing thirty pounds in six months. In business it could be doubling profitability in a year. For a sales executive the goal might be to add 50 per cent to their sales commission or income within a year.

Think in advance about the difficulties you may face and how you can overcome them. Your challenge may be the most exciting thing you have ever done, but other people's perceptions can be very different. You need to be upfront with everyone who will be affected by your plans.

You also need to be sure that you really want to do it. Transformation in anything, not just your golf game, is difficult. Do you really want to slog away at the range or putting green when your back is hurting or you're cold and wet? Will you keep going even when your improvement plateaus, no matter how hard you're working and practising? If you haven't got a burning desire to improve your golf, lose weight, double your income or save the business, then you won't see it through – it's as simple as that.

I had a huge and longstanding desire to prove to myself that I could have been a contender. I was reaching out to that fifteen-year-old version of myself who saw Seve Ballesteros tear up the course in Royal Dublin in 1982. I wanted to prove that I had the talent to be a decent golfer. For me, that was a pretty strong motivator.

If you do have the desire, then you must keep it at the forefront of your mind. You must go all out to make sure that you live and breathe it. One of the easiest ways to do this is by making your challenge public. From my experience and that of several friends and clients, I think that you're much more likely to succeed if you make your big promise public.

2. Create a very strong push or away-from motivation

This is the golfing equivalent of having a picture of you at your fattest on the fridge door. It's about making sure you have something from which you strongly want to move away. At the most extreme, it's about feeling a sense of disgust about where you are now.

Whether internally or at the top of your voice, you need to be shouting, 'Enough! I've had it with this. No more.' That's the point I had reached when I shot 110 on my annual visit to the golf course back in 2003. It was humiliating. I made a decision either to give golf up, or to get really good at it. Whatever happened, I decided that I was never going to shoot a round of golf in the hundreds again.

There is no doubt that we're all motivated in slightly different ways. Some people, arguably the healthy ones, are motivated more strongly by a moving towards or pull goal. They can look at the picture of the fancy house or the Ferrari and use that as their motivation to work hard and make their dreams a reality. They don't have to twist the knife of dissatisfaction.

Sadly, though, that kind of motivation only works for a third of us. For those of us in the remaining two-thirds the stronger motivation is wanting to move away from existing pain or future pain. We need to twist the knife to cause enough pain to force us to take action. Or we need to envisage the catastrophes that will take place in the future if we don't act now – visualise the bailiffs arriving at the front door before we actually deal with our credit · card debt; think about how making staff redundant would feel before making the necessary fundamental change to the business; experience a serious health problem before we're able to ease off the cake and hit the treadmill.

The understanding of these two motivational factors is what allows you to create the magic and get going. If you can bring both of them together in your mind at the same time you will be almost invincible. And I say almost because without the third critical factor you'll still never get properly started.

 JOHN'S TRUE STORIES

During my challenge, especially in the dead of winter, there were a number of nights when I really couldn't be bothered to get out and practise. I had to balance my challenge with fifty-hour weeks at our garden centres and my efforts still to be a decent husband and father. So I used to come home from work, cook dinner, give my daughter her bath and then read her a story.

After that, the last thing I wanted to do was to drag my sorry backside up to the range. Especially if I'd already been there earlier in the day without any great progress. So often I'd pour a glass of wine and slump on to the sofa, telling myself that a night off wouldn't do any harm. But then I'd start to think about all those keyboard warriors who had told me the challenge was impossible and continued to taunt me at every stage when my scores slipped (I was blogging about the challenge on various internet forums). Imagining hearing them tell me they were right and that they'd told me so all along had me leaping out of my seat, ignoring the glass of wine and running to the car more effectively than any dreams of achieving that glorious round.

. . . .

3. Belief that your challenge or endeavour is possible

At corporate events, when I'm talking about the *Dream On* challenge, I'm generally asked two questions: 'What is your standard of play now?' and 'what is the big secret that you discovered during the year?'

The interesting thing about the second question is that it disregards the fact that – as we all instinctively know – there is no one thing, no secret. Ben Hogan never did dig up an ancient golfing scroll at the bottom of the garden at a rented house in St Andrews which told him to tweak his right thumb just before impact.

For me the secret was, and still is, belief. I can plot the ups and downs of my golf challenge against the ups and downs of my belief in my likelihood of succeeding and see two almost identical graphs, with the belief line slightly ahead of the score line. To begin with my confidence and belief were high. I really didn't think that it would be all that difficult to achieve the challenge. I was eminently capable of batting away all the internet trolls who told me it was impossible. I was even capable of batting away the advice of golfing stars like Darren Clarke and Sam Torrance.

As such, my scores consistently improved. But then I'd have a few rough rounds, or sustain an injury, and my belief would ebb a little. And then my scores would stop improving, my belief would decrease, and my scores would worsen again.

Then, out of the blue, I'd read an inspirational article which would fire me up. Or I'd meet someone with knowledge of the game, or someone I particularly respected, and my glass of belief would fill to the brim again. And then the magic would happen. I'd shoot my best round for weeks, and the glass would start overflowing. For a while I'd shoot great rounds, shift to a new level of scoring. Perhaps shooting rounds in the low rather than high seventies.

To really make yourself click into action, you must use all three of these steps together. You need to learn to spin them in your mind, and, when you do, it becomes almost impossible to not take focused action towards your goal. Learn to fill up your glass of belief with the tales of people who have achieved what you want to do.

 ## JOHN'S TRUE STORIES

The single most important moment for me in terms of building my golf belief was the story of Bob Macdermott. Bob was a single-figure handicap golfer who suffered a dreadful accident and lost his left leg, left arm and the thumb on his right hand. But he is the most determined person I have ever come across. With a huge amount of work and new prosthetic limbs, Bob created a new swing. He now plays off scratch and holds the course record of 66 at his local club.

His story had a huge impact on me when I was undertaking the challenge. I'd been scoring badly and was feeling sorry for myself due to problems with wrist pain and mildly arthritic hips. Reading Bob's story made my own tribulations pale into insignificance. Even countenancing the idea that my own challenge was impossible went completely out the window when I saw what Bob had achieved.

. . . .

THE FIFTY TIPS

Over the past three years I've collected hundreds of tips that I felt would be perfect for the book – narrowing them down to just fifty has been a remarkably difficult task but a vital one, because I wanted to make sure that I included only the very best tips, the ones that actually work. I'm acutely aware that this is a highly subjective list – but these are the principles and tips that have been truly effective for me and the many golfers I have worked with.

While I hope you will find all of the tips incredibly useful, you should pay particular attention to the first 10 and the underlying core principles. These super tips – uber tips, cornerstone tips, call them what you will – represent the ten most important concepts in a golf improvement programme.

1. Don't trust – measure and make your own mind up

One of the golf tips that I remember most clearly from my childhood – to such an extent that it hardwired itself into my brain – is: '*You'll always get closer to the pin from the fringe of the green with a putter instead of a wedge.*' The extension of this is the idea that you'll always get closer with a little chip and run, using a less lofted club, than you will by getting the ball in the air with a wedge and attempting to pitch close.

When I started the challenge, I treated this tip as gospel. The problem was that I always struggled to putt from the edge of a putting green. My club always seemed to snag and I could never work out how hard to strike to get the ball past the longer grass section of green, then to slow down enough on the main putting surface. The result was that I was either putting past the hole or coming up very short. This golden rule that should have improved my scoring was having the reverse effect.

I felt like a bit of a heretic when I started using my seven iron from the edge, but the difference in my scoring was like night and day. And therein lies the lesson. You must take the conventional wisdom with a pinch of salt. Nearly every part of the game has been played differently by some great champion or other. What I say, or what a golf journalist attempting to fill his quota that month might say, is worthless unless you can prove that it actually works for you.

For a while, I continued using a chipping action with a nine iron from off the green until I noticed that lots of pros were actually using their lob wedges for this shot – and landing the ball much closer to the hole. I also read a quote from the great Chi-Chi Rodríguez: 'There are no bumps in the air' – making the point that he always wanted to get the ball high with as little run as possible on the green. That made a lot of sense to me.

So, what was right for me? My putting versus chipping test had, up to this point, been entirely qualitative and I wanted a little more evidence for these longer shots. So one evening I visited the par three course at Blackwood and conducted a simple experiment. I took out my trusty sand wedge and, with a classic 'wristy' pitching style, hit twenty-one balls to the hole from about fifteen yards. I walked up and kicked away the ten balls closest to the hole and measured the distance between the eleventh ball and the cup. I repeated the exercise with a fixed wrist chipping motion, this time using my nine iron, and again I measured how far the eleventh ball was from the hole.

Amazingly I had pitched the ball on average more than six inches closer to the hole. Was this just luck? I repeated the exercise with another two sets of twenty-one balls – with exactly the same results, to the inch.

The benefits of this test were twofold. Not only had I improved my short game but I was also now able to approach all tips and words of wisdom with a new attitude and perspective. I still read and listened to as much advice as possible, but knew that I could conclusively prove whether or not that advice worked for me.

In the early days of my challenge I wasted a lot of time believing that every 'secret' I came across would transform my game. It's very easy to trust someone who is better at the game than you are, or indeed a golf instructional programme with a great team of advertising copywriters. It's when you can take that tip or piece of advice and test it yourself that you give yourself an exceptional advantage.

This advantage comes in the form of confidence on the course. Once I'd completed my initial tests from the fringe I knew, with quantifiable evidence, that I would consistently get better results with a chipping motion from this area. Likewise, I knew that a pitching action with my sand wedge, from almost anywhere else around the green, would nearly always yield the best outcome. That confidence, when standing over the ball, increased my ability to strike the ball well, especially from a less-than-perfect lie.

So, regardless of how compelling any tip sounds to you, or how much sense it might make, test everything and see the results yourself, with your own scores, before you make it a permanent part of how you play.

I'm entirely self-taught. It's a good way to learn, but you do have moments of frustration and confusion. To fix that, I took seven years' worth of *Golf Digest*s and divided them into stacks on my kitchen table. I went through every one and wrote down every distance tip I came across. It took a while, and when I'd finished I had 397 tips. I eliminated all of the duplications, then I went to work dealing with the tips that conflicted – stance, grip pressure, wrist cock, and so on. All of the contradictions I put to the test. Using each tip, I noted the balls that I absolutely murdered. Tips that produced a ball in the 'kill' column made the final list, which resides in a little black book I carry wherever I go. I call it the Bible.

SEAN FISTER – National Long Drive Champion

2. Own your own swing

Golfwise, I did it all by myself. I'm not indebted to anybody for the game I've got. That's my single biggest source of satisfaction.

LEE TREVINO

There is no one way to play the game. Look at all the great swings in the game and they're all different. Everyone has their own swing and their own way and their own different body types ... You can play it with hands, you can play it with all body, you can play it with anywhere in between. You can play it right side, you can play it left side. You have to find a system that works for you. Whatever makes your game better, do it. If you hit the ball better and you hit the ball consistently better, do it.

TIGER WOODS

There are plenty of overzealous teaching pros out there who would disagree with me about this. I've met several 'stack and tilt' teaching pros, who insist that their swing is 'perfect' and 'right'. But, as Tiger says, do whatever works best for you.

It's now that I'll drag out the obvious example: Jim Furyk's swing, famously described by Gary McCord as looking like 'a one-armed golfer using an axe to kill a snake in a telephone booth'. It's an extreme example, but out on the tour, even at the very highest level, you'll see that all players swing the club slightly differently.

All the players do share the same fundamentals, though. They nearly all start with a similar stance, grip, balance and alignment. And most of the time their positions at impact, even Jim Furyk's, are startlingly similar.

There is a fundamental difference, however, between owning your own swing and simply adopting your natural swing. If you insist on keeping a swing that creates a fundamental flaw, such as a slice or a hook, then you're jeopardising your long-term potential to score well. The secret is to use great advice to fix that natural flaw without trying to adopt a swing which will never feel natural.

We all have 'natural' swings. The problem is, a natural swing produces a slice. That's because the homunculus, the part of the brain that controls motor movement, sees the hands as the largest part of the anatomy. When you're a baby you're constantly moving your hands away from your body so you can explore things in your environment. Now, when the day comes to play golf, the instinct to move your hands away from you really takes over. On the downswing the hands move away from the body too soon, out toward the target line, and you end up cutting across the ball from out to in. Thanks to the homunculus, I make a very good living.

BOB TOSKI

3. Keep it simple (but annoyingly, of course, it's not quite as simple as that ...)

If you can't explain it to a six year old, you don't understand it yourself ... Everything should be made as simple as possible, but not simpler.

ALBERT EINSTEIN

One day I will find the right words, and they will be simple.

JACK KEROUAC

Golf is a complex game. Coupled with this is the fact that practically all teaching of the game comes from a single perspective of one generally intelligent and well-meaning coach. And that teaching will have developed from their own learning and teaching style at least as much as it will have from the results they get from their students.

One of the simplest concepts to help you understand your own learning is the 'Why, What, How, What If?' model.

'Why' learners want to know why they should care – why they should be learning this, why it is important, why focus on it now.

'What' learners want the facts without padding. They need step-by-step processes. They like working with people who come to the conversation prepared, so having an agenda is useful. The bottom line for them is 'What do I need to know?'

'How' learners need to see the relationship between what they are learning and the big picture. They want to see the relationships and connections between the new information and what they already know. Give them context and show how what you are teaching them is similar to something they already understand or know how to do.

'What If' learners want to discuss alternatives with you. They'll ask questions about why it is done the way you outline and whether another way is better. They need to understand the boundaries and the issues that were considered in making the decision to do it this way. They can be a little frustrating to teach because they seem to veer into unrelated areas and have a hard time staying on topic. But this is how they learn. You need to allow them to ask a few questions and let them roll around the possibilities in their heads. They may give you some creative ideas you never would have thought of.

So how did all this affect me during my challenge? Well, I have a tendency to move into the 'What If' category. This can distract me and take away my focus. And it often causes me to become too theoretical. That means it's extremely important for me not to dig too deep into the neuroscience of improvement, or some of the deeper theories, unless I've specifically proven to myself that they work with measurable results. So, to an extent, you can see that Tip 1 – Don't trust, measure – is almost as much a reminder to me as it is a cornerstone for you.

And how does this apply to you? Well, you have to understand that your own golf improvement will be governed by your own learning style. You'll need to find teachers, coaches, tips and tools that can work for your style of learning. But make sure you don't restrict your learning capacity by putting yourself entirely into one category. Be aware of how you learn and then think about how you could improve by adopting characteristics from other categories.

'What' learners won't even have read this far! They won't be able to grasp anything that doesn't relate to a simple process – the potential next step that they can take out on the range or the golf course on their very next visit. There's nothing wrong with that: ultimately all that matters is getting yourself into a position where you can produce quantifiable improvements.

So, if you can, try to position yourself within some of these categories – and treat the rest of the tips, or your ability to obtain an overall improvement within your own game, with a more open mind. A mind that can accept that if you focus on learning as effectively as possible, then you'll improve more quickly. What remains crucial, though, to paraphrase the Einstein quote at the beginning, is that you keep your learning as simple as possible.

4. Fix your flaws

You've probably heard of the 80/20 rule before. It sits at the core of my golf improvement process and I will look at the theory a little more in Tip 7. The principle applies to pretty much everything that happens in our lives. In essence what it says is that 20 per cent of the work you do creates 80 per cent of the results. When it comes to golf, this means that 20 per cent of the work that you do to get better will produce 80 per cent of the improvement results. Just keeping this in mind will help your practising enormously.

Where it most applies though is in the acceptance that you have certain natural flaws within your game that are extremely difficult to get rid of. And if you can concentrate on fixing these, you'll make an enormous improvement to your overall scoring. For me, the key issues are an overly strong right-hand grip and a tendency to have an 'out-to-in' swing. The latter is something that I share with about 95 per cent of amateur golfers.

If I allow them back into my swing, these are the things that will make me shoot the big scores. If I start to slice or pull the ball, as a result of the swing, I'm going to stand on the tee with no idea of whether I'll be hitting it badly left or right. That's an incredibly easy way to shoot a mid, or even high, eighties round rather a low seventies one. And that's exactly what can happen to me.

But if I can hit the ball straight, my game comes together and, if my short game doesn't let me down, I have the chance to pull an epic round out of the bag. So, if I want to shoot low scores consistently, I need to get my natural swing flaws under control. They are, without a doubt, the biggest block for me in terms of shooting a low round. And that's why I must always ensure that I go straight back to fixing those issues when they start to crop up. I need to ignore the practice that I'd like to do (short game generally) and work through the drills that cure the over-the-top motion.

If you watch professionals at the range before a tournament, many of them are working very hard on the fundamentals of the game. They're working on their stance, alignment, grip and swing path – just what you should be doing in practice. And their coaches are standing behind them checking and double-checking that they're not moving fractionally out of their perfect 'slot' and back towards their natural flaws. English golfer Paul Casey has often said that a huge amount of his practice revolves around making sure that he isn't reverting back to the swing he had in his early teens.

So you need to identify, either by yourself or with a golf professional, the flaws in your swing and then the drills or the tips to get rid of them. Obviously there are lots of them in this book, but a good pro will give you good drills too. A bad pro won't, though. They'll just tell you to swing more like 'this' or make sure not to put your hands in 'that' position – useless advice. You need drills and specific actions that you can take to the range and use. And if the pro fails to provide those, then move on. Quickly!

Then you must prioritise fixing that flaw to the exclusion of anything else. You need to put the time in at the range to ensure that you've sorted out that problem, so that the next time you're playing, you can stand at the first tee with a strong sense of confidence that your slice, shank, hook, pull, push – whatever – has gone. It's rarely as hard as you might expect, but it does require some work – and the acceptance of the fact that it won't be fixed with a new driver or some sort of clever teaching aid that promises to do it all for you.

5. Be willing to put in some hard work

Golf teaching at all levels is blighted by the power of the idea of the magic tip or secret. But in reality, the secret doesn't exist. It took me until my mid-thirties to grasp the fact that – rather than being the holders of the magic secret – my sporting heroes were, almost without exception, the hardest working guys in their field. I was a huge Formula One fan in my twenties and, like most fans, was obsessed with Ayrton Senna. He was the Seve Ballesteros, George Best or Muhammad Ali of Formula One – in possession of a talent that seemed otherworldly at times, especially in wet conditions. It's easy to assume these guys are of a different genetic make-up to the rest of us but that's simply not true – this assumption is nothing more than a convenient excuse for avoiding extremely hard work.

I watched a documentary about Senna and two facts hit home. Firstly I discovered that when he was a kart racer as a child he was pretty rubbish at racing in the wet. So much so that when it rained he would perform badly and lose the race. Humiliating loss didn't sit well with Ayrton Senna – even as a child. So he chose to change the situation: every time it started raining, he'd run to his kart and practise as much as possible. He forced himself to develop the skills that I had naively assumed were simply part of his make-up.

The second fact to emerge was his running regime

– in fact, the documentary showed extensive footage of him running on a dusty track. He would pound away, wearing through countless pairs of trainers every year. Hard solitary work in an effort to give himself that slight edge over his rivals.

This new knowledge about Senna, coupled with an understanding that Seve's incredible short game was the result of endless evenings experimenting with his brother's three iron, made me realise that there is a price to pay for excellence – and it's a lot of hard work. That's a great thing. It allows the likes of you and me to make an attempt at getting really, really good at some sport or other endeavour. This understanding enabled me to set out on my own golf challenge with a certain level of confidence. I had recognised that Seve's and Senna's successes weren't just the result of God-given talent – the hard work they'd put in had been at least as important.

I set about creating a strategy that would allow me to focus on overcoming problems and integrating the solutions into my game, so that I could effectively remove any problems or swing flaws that had arisen. I wanted to leave as little to chance as possible. It took me more than half the year to develop the following formula, but it proved invaluable.

1. Diagnose problem

2. Take initial measurement

3. Look for or create solution

4. Create or find drill to put solution in place and consistently work at it

5. Measure again

6. Repeat the drill as necessary until it is fixed or the new technique is in place.

Placing the goal of improvement into this type of process helped me enormously. It allowed me to see the overall goal as less of a vast mountain to climb and more of a set of smaller peaks to overcome.

To illustrate how this strategy helped to solve a real problem of mine, I should tell you about my excessive lower body movement, or 'Elvis legs' as my pro called them. To start with, I'd go to the range and take some measurements with my normal swing: I'd hit about ten balls and measure how many of them fell between two markers in the distance. Then I'd start drilling. The first drill I found to help with my Elvis legs was the 'feet together drill', which is exactly as it sounds. I'd strike about twenty balls with my feet tight together (so my lower body was forced to be still) then take another ten shots, measuring their quality with my 'perfect strike' scale.

When I'd completed that drill, I still noticed I had excessive leg movement so I tried another one. I placed my bag against my right hip in an effort to control any sway. I hit another twenty balls, and by the end of both of these drill processes I had dramatically stilled my lower body.

JOHN'S TRUE STORIES

. . . .

When I was growing up in Portstewart, Darren Clarke was fast developing a reputation as an extraordinarily talented young golfer. Darren was quite the bon viveur in those days and it's an image that he still presents strongly. But it's important to realise that he's also an incredibly hard working pro.

A cousin of mine and Darren are members at Royal Portrush. A few years ago, around Christmas time, when we had a lot of snow in Northern Ireland, the club bar was full of people – including my cousin – sheltering from the elements and enjoying a fair amount of Christmas cheer. The course was covered in snow and deserted, as was the practice facility. Apart from one man. One solitary golfer out there practising in the snow. He had cleared a little area and practised his chipping. For three solid hours ...

The solitary golfer was the best golfer in the club. It was Darren Clarke. Most of us would imagine that he would have been inside, drinking Guinness and holding court, but, in fact, he was out in the freezing cold working on his short game – paying the price.

. . . .

'Practising all the time helps my confidence more than it does my swing. Knowing you've paid a price gives you a big advantage.'

LEE TREVINO

6. Be honest about your abilities

We can deceive ourselves in lots of different ways – just go to Wikipedia and search for 'cognitive biases'. I've been involved in the entrepreneurial business world for over 25 years and I think I've seen nearly every single one of the entries on this list exhibited by business owners (including myself). Golfers do exactly the same thing. We endlessly fool ourselves and tell ourselves stories that aren't strictly true about our own behaviour.

There are two cognitive biases that stand out for me, although they have a variety of different names and are closely linked. The first of these is a confirmation bias, or a predisposition to see only validation: a tendency to search for ways to confirm what we believe about ourselves or our theories. We look for things that allow us to say, 'See, I was right about that!'

In a golfing context, this bias allows us either to assume we're better or that we're worse than we are. If a golfer with confirmation bias hits a few bad putts, he'll say, 'I've never been able to putt' or, if he's incredibly confident by nature, he'll claim to be the best in the world after a few good shots.

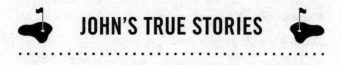

JOHN'S TRUE STORIES

During my challenge, I was playing a round of golf with my friend and regular playing partner Stuart Kennedy. Stuart was playing well that day and needed about a twelve-foot putt to win the hole. He strode up to the ball and stroked it home. As he swaggered across to pick it out of the hole, he said 'See, I don't miss many of those.' The facts would absolutely not bear that out. The best golfers in the world only make about 50 per cent of six-foot putts, and here was Stuart trying to convince me that he was a better player than the average pro. The truth of the matter is that he is a great putter, but that's as much to do with his attitude as anything else.

This is confirmation bias at its very best. If you can stand over a twelve-foot putt and think, whether it's true or not, that you're more than likely to get it in, well, you're vastly more likely to succeed than the tentative golfer who stands over the ball, thinking 'I'm rubbish at this distance.'

. . . .

The second critical bias is one often described as 'emotional estimation', meaning that we tend to be controlled by our emotions when we're making decisions. This bias can manifest itself in the following ways.

- We ignore the fact that we rarely manage to produce a decent draw and take on the corner on the tricky dog leg. We pull it out of bounds.

- We see a tiny gap in the trees and imagine that we're a Mickelson/Woods/Ballesteros golfing superhero. Standing, with our golfing superhero underpants outside our trousers, we know we can hit the ball through that gap, over the river so that it lands six inches from the hole. We clatter into the trees.

- Our playing partner hits his nine iron to within two feet of the flag. We have 135 yards to the pin and know that we once hit our nine iron 135 yards so attempt to do the same thing again. Even though we know, if we'd listen to our logical brain, that we always take an eight iron and nine times out of ten it's the right club. The result? Landing short of the green.

You get the picture. I could easily rattle off ten scenarios like that and you'd probably have to admit that you'd experienced eight of them. We are all so illogical when it comes to golf that it's hilarious at times. I really wonder if there's another sport out there that produces such bizarre behaviour in otherwise rational human beings.

The great thing is that there's a solution. The cornerstone of my business coaching and consulting consists of two key concepts.

1. Finding out exactly how good or bad the company is to begin with

What are the key figures (or Key Performance Indicators in management guff) for the last few weeks that the company has produced? Very often I have to wade through endless emotional estimation before I can find the actual truth, but finding the truth is absolutely essential if I'm to help the firm make rapid progress forward.

2. Putting in place a new weekly measurement system for these KPIs

Ensure that all parties are aware of the progress, and make the people who control them report the results back to the powers that be. They use a simple email template that essentially says something along the lines of:

- Here are my KPIs for this week.

- This is what I'm going to do to improve that figure for next week.

- Here are the results of the actions I took during the week as a result of last week's KPIs.

That's it in a nutshell. But enough of my justification for being paid as a consultant. The relevant point for this book is that this very simple process applies to almost any form of improvement and it's incredibly powerful when applied to your golf. If you focus purely on the facts, then you can sweep all biases to one side. You can focus on the reality of exactly where you are and set a very clear target for where you want to go. And if you dig deep into your KPIs, you'll be able to produce the equivalent of that weekly reporting email that works so well in business.

The process starts with your first control round. To begin with, all you need is the total score and total number of putts. This information allows you to put the score on the wall and think, 'That's it, that's the beginning and if I really focus I'll never consistently shoot a terrible score like that again.' It goes without saying that this round of golf must have no mulligans, no gimmes, no preferred lies and obviously no creative accounting. It doesn't matter how bad it is. It just is. Remember, you're removing the emotion from your scores!

If you can, though, you should spend a little time analysing that card. Imagine you're that tedious bore at the bar who insists on reliving every hole from their round with anyone who will listen. Except keep it to yourself and see if you can find what is causing you the 'big miss'. What is making you hit the double or treble bogies? You probably know what your big flaw is, but now is the time to address it and, as we discuss in 'Fix your flaws' (Tip 4), start to repair it.

From now on, you need to keep all your cards and note the decrease in your scores. A simple graph on a spreadsheet allows you to plot your overall score and number of putts. To take this process further, work on three further measurements as often as possible.

- Score 21 balls hit from 50 yards and out, and measure their proximity to the hole. The target is to get these within three feet, on average.

- Score 21 balls from 15 yards, and again measure their proximity to the hole. The aim is to get these within one foot, on average.

- Score 12 putts in a clockface pattern, six feet from the hole, and attempt to hole more than 50 per cent per cent of them. If you can achieve this, you're putting as well as a touring professional so it's not an easy task.

These three scores are a superb measure of how good your short game is. Dave Pelz has a dramatically more detailed short game handicap system, but it's so complex that it's almost impossible to persuade anyone to complete it on a regular basis. My three scores system can be completed in about twenty minutes, whenever you've access to a green, and it provides an excellent way to chart your progress in the critical areas that will help lower your scores.

With four golfing KPIs, and an internal reporting system, you can transport yourself to a different planet to most of your golfing friends, who will continue to be at the mercy of their emotions and cognitive biases.

 ## JOHN'S TRUE STORIES

During my challenge I delayed my putting practice for far too long. I allowed myself to get distracted by various other more exciting parts of the game, especially distance off the tee. I even found myself visiting the gym several times a week as a distraction.

Then one day I shot a 90 and discovered that I'd taken 40 putts. Even more ridiculously that score included eight three-putts. I blogged about this and received a tirade of abuse from a well-meaning but frustrated supporter. He told me I was 'just like all other golfers' and would never get close to shooting par unless I worked hard on my putting.

This was like a red rag to a bull and a great example of the 'away from' motivation in action. I could imagine the (entirely justifiable) abuse I would receive if I failed in my challenge and never fully addressed my poor putting performance. So I spent 35 hours in one week working on my putting and went out the next weekend and took exactly 28 putts during a round, so in one week I took 12 strokes off my previous score.

Obviously that was an exceptional week of putting, and I hadn't often taken 40 putts – but it's a wonderful example of how, if you focus on the numbers, the KPIs, and then take action to improve them, you can make an enormous difference to your scores.

. . . .

7. The magic of 80/20

The 80/20 rule is something that I came across many years ago in a book by Richard Koch, *The 80/20 Principle*. The core principle is that 80 per cent of our results flow from just 20 per cent of what we do. And this theory applies to everything.

In the business world this means all sorts of fascinating things. 20 per cent of our customers provide 80 per cent of the sales; 20 per cent of our employees create 80 per cent of the human resource problems; 20 per cent of our marketing spend creates 80 per cent of the new customers.

If you would like to improve an area of your life, look hard for the 20 per cent that is producing 80 per cent of the results and focus on that. You can quickly improve your outcomes.

80/20 gets a little more complex than that, though. There are sub levels. The best way to explain this is to use a road traffic analogy. 20 per cent of the roads in your area will carry 80 per cent of the traffic. But that 20 per cent is also subject to the principle. That means that 20 per cent of that top 20 per cent will carry 80 per cent of the 80 per cent of the traffic. In other words 4 per cent will carry 64 per cent of the traffic on the roads, and so on …

This principle can dramatically improve your golf scoring. Let's take the way you practise at the range. I've spent hundreds and hundreds of hours at the range working on my own game and observing how others practise. In general, as you well know, most practice simply involves golfers hitting the ball as far as they can down the range. As such, a tremendous amount of practice is simply wasted effort. But if you work on a little drill at the same time to sharpen your fifty-yard pitches, and nail a couple of these during the next round to save yourself two shots – that's 80/20 loosely in action.

My fascination with this rule came about from trying to work out the most effective things I could do to save myself strokes. Taking a hundred different improvement methods, what were the twenty that would make the biggest difference? Could I just ignore the other eighty? What was the sub layer below that? What were the four things I could do that would cause the most improvement for the least effort?

Discovering that twenty, and ideally the four, will radically change your ability to improve. For me course management stood out above all others. If you can methodically plot your way round a golf course and avoid trouble then you'll get an instant improvement in your scores and it won't have cost you a penny.

The second key realisation for me was that short game practice, particularly within the fifty yards range, was going to make a huge difference. Sixty to 70 per cent of the shots you take will be from 100 yards and in, so improvement in that zone can make an enormous difference.

My third crucial point is one that has been highlighted by Mark Broadie, a professor at Columbia Business

School. He spent much of the last decade logging 70,000 shots that were hit by players of all levels and ages, from tour pros to 100-shooters and discovered that much of the 'drive for show and putt for dough' cliché wasn't true. So many golfers waste so many shots by being wild off the tee, and by using six-irons to hit the ball on to the greens, rather than a wedge. In other words, a long straight drive is vital to your scoring.

For me, and the 6,300-yard course that I was using for my challenge, this information meant I could focus on three things and hopefully end up with a game that could produce the perfect round. I was already hitting the ball a long way but I needed to straighten it up. A number of the tips in here show how I did that. I needed to get really good from 100 yards and in, because if I was driving the ball properly I'd be right in this zone, and accuracy from this range would provide birdie opportunities on a number of the holes. And, finally, I needed to make sure that my six-foot putts were as good as possible, to give myself a chance of holing out when I managed to fire it close.

You'll see how a number of the tips in this book relate to these goals. You'll also understand why two hours on the par three and one on the range with my driver was vastly more efficient than four hours spent slogging round the main course playing 18 holes. That was the 80/20 process that I went through with my own game and personal improvement – if you can find your own twenty, or narrow right down to four, then you'll make your own dramatic improvements.

I also suggest that you ignore the 80 per cent of your practice that you know will only make a marginal improvement. For me, the most obvious example of that was learning how to shape the ball. Blackwood is a relatively straight course. There was no need for me to be able to produce wonderful fades and draws. It might have looked pretty, and would probably have helped on a couple of holes, but it would have required a tremendous amount of practice – time that I didn't have.

 ## JOHN'S TRUE STORIES

During the challenge, I came across Richard Asher, from South Africa, who was trying to go from being an average golfer to someone who could play at a US Masters-winning standard. Richard asked numerous pros, including Darren Clarke, for their best advice. Darren told him to do nothing but chip and putt for six months and then spend about 90 per cent of his time on his short game – most of the pros spend 75 per cent of their time on their short game and he could never understand why most amateurs don't do the same.

That's 80/20. Clarke is explaining exactly what is in the 20 per cent that makes the difference. When did you last see an amateur golfer spending 75% of their practice time on short game?

8. Go to the movies in your mind

Competitive golf is played mainly on a five-and-a-half-inch course ... the space between your ears.

BOBBY JONES

Major James Nesmeth had a dream of improving his golf game – and he developed a unique method of achieving his goal. Until he devised this method, he was just your average weekend golfer, shooting in mid-to low-nineties. Then, for seven years, he completely quit the game. Never touched a club. Never set foot on a fairway.

Ironically, it was during this seven-year break from the game that Major Nesmeth came up with his amazingly effective technique for improving his game – a technique we can all learn from. In fact, the first time he set foot on a golf course after his hiatus from the game, he shot an astonishing 74! He had cut 20 strokes off his average without having swung a golf club in seven years! Unbelievable. Not only that, but his physical condition had actually deteriorated during those seven years. What was Major Nesmeth's secret? Visualization! You see, Major Nesmeth had spent those seven years as a prisoner of war in North Vietnam. During those seven years, he was imprisoned in a cage that was approximately four and one-half feet high and five feet long.

During almost the entire time he was imprisoned, he saw no one, talked to no one and experienced no physical activity. During the first few months he did virtually nothing but hope and pray for his release. Then he realized he had to find some way to occupy his mind or he would lose his sanity and probably his life. That's when he learned to visualize.

In his mind, he selected his favorite golf course and started playing golf. Every day, he played a full 18 holes at the imaginary country club of his dreams. He experienced everything to the last detail. He saw himself dressed in his golfing clothes. He smelled the fragrance of the trees and the freshly trimmed grass. He experienced different weather conditions – windy spring days, overcast winter days, and sunny summer mornings. In his imagination, every detail of the tee, the individual blades of grass, the trees, the singing birds, the scampering squirrels and the lay of the course became totally real.

He felt the grip of the club in his hands. He instructed himself as he practised smoothing out his down-swing and the follow-through on his shot. Then he watched the ball arc down the exact center of the fairway, bounce a couple of times and roll to the exact spot he had selected, all in his mind. In the real world, he was in no hurry. He had no place to go. So in his mind he took every step on his way to the ball, just as if he were physically on the course. It took him just as long in imaginary time to play eighteen holes as it would have taken in reality. Not a detail was omitted. Not once did he ever miss a shot, never a hook or a slice, never a missed putt. Seven days a week. Four hours a day. Eighteen holes. Seven years. Twenty strokes off. Shot a seventy-four.

A Second Helping of Chicken Soup for the Soul
JACK CANFIELD AND MARK VICTOR HANSEN

I didn't come across Major Nesmeth's story until the end of my challenge, but it had a great impact on me. Not least because, even before I had read the story, I had been trying to play the course in my mind every night before I went to sleep. I worked hard to make my imagined round as realistic as possible but shot par on every hole. I would play in varying wind conditions and make sure that the round played was subtly different each time. But I still shot par. I didn't visualise myself playing outlandishly brilliant golf but I also never struck a bad shot.

I would do things differently now, though. I often fell asleep before I completed the (harder) back nine, so they didn't get anything like as much mental practice as the front nine. I also had a tendency to play either just the front nine holes if I was nipping up for a quick round, or even just the first six. As a result I was more confident on the first nine holes, and this became a problem for me.

The quest for my pars, and the restrictions that I created in my imagination, also caused me problems in the later stages. I felt, foolishly and erroneously as it turned out, that I would have to play the round at something very close to par on each hole. My belief didn't extend to my ability to be able to rattle off a few birdies or even an eagle to save me from a couple of bogeys or even a double bogey.

This meant that, in the late stages of my challenge, when I could have been playing my challenge-winning round, I gave up if I slipped to three over par because I felt that I didn't have the game to pull me back. I was helped by sports psychologist David Walters at this point: David works extensively with soldiers who have returned from combat with horrendous cases of Post Traumatic Stress Disorder having witnessed terrible scenes of killing and death. So dealing with a bit of golfer 'trauma' was hardly much of an issue for him! He reminded me that I had birdied every hole on the course at some point and that I needed to believe that I could string a few birdies together if that was necessary. But the damage was mostly done with the visualisation, I feel. If I had visualised the birdies as a regular part of my game, this could only have helped.

Many people feel that they cannot visualise but this

simply isn't the case. If I were to ask you the colour of your front door and the position of its handle, you could immediately visualise your front door in order to answer the question. Likewise, if I asked you not to think about pink elephants, you would find it almost impossible not to have a pink elephant in your mind. So we *can* all do it, but it's a skill that comes more easily to some people than others.

You can use visualisation in many different ways. To motivate you, you might want to visualise your playing partner's face when you beat him, or the feeling you'll get when you reach your goal or win the monthly medal. Focus on the feeling as much if not more than the image, and make it crystal clear. Make sure your images have vivid colour too.

Someone who used visualisation to great effect was Jack Nicklaus. He never played a shot physically until he had seen the full shot in his head. He would start with the ball in his mind in the perfect part of the fairway and see it play backwards in his mind all the way to the tee. He had a clear image in his mind of exactly what he expected of the shot before he started his backswing. So Jack was firing off the signals to the muscles to perform the shot before he hit the shot. This really is a superb way to improve your golf for no time on the range.

My biggest visualisation success was and is with Seve and his short game. Before every putt, pitch and chip I imagine his grip on the club and see him taking the shot before I do. Then I just slip into that image of his body.

JOHN'S TRUE STORIES

Nine months after my challenge Stephen Watson of the BBC asked to meet me and play a single hole at a local course. This was part of a series in which he played one very difficult or famous par three hole with the interviewee and conducted the interview at the same time.

My game had slipped quite a lot by this stage. I'd broken a couple of ribs not long after completing the challenge, and then, when winter came along, it became very important to me to spend time with my family and make up for all those lost evenings and weekends at the range. By the time the phone call came I hadn't picked up a club for several months. I was nervous, to say the least.

I had no opportunity to get to the range the day before, so I had to do all my preparation mentally the night before. The hole we played was quite famous – the par three 16th at Belvoir golf club in Belfast – so it was easy to find images online of the view from the tee.

I simply sat and visualised playing a perfect hybrid off the tee over and over again. The hole was a little over two hundred yards long, the perfect distance for this club. I spent about an hour doing this and then repeated the exercise in my car as I drove the half an hour to the course.

When I got there, the view was very similar to what I'd been visualising but we were playing it at a closer tee. So my hybrid was out of the picture and I had to use my four iron. I replayed the perfect shot over again a few times in my head, stepped up and struck it. The ball missed the flag by about an inch and ran past.

That's how well visualisation works for me.

I feel that hitting specific shots – playing the ball to a certain place in a certain way – is 50 per cent mental picture, 40 per cent setup, and 10 per cent swing.

. . . .

My last thought before I take the club away isn't a thought at all. It's a picture, a visualisation, a sensation. If I think of swinging slowly, my last thought isn't 'swing slowly'. It's an image of me swinging slowly.

JACK NICKLAUS

9. Understand practice and the science behind it

This is a great exercise from Daniel Coyle's excellent book, *The Talent Code*. Take a few seconds to look at each of the following lists, spending the same amount of time on each one.

A	B
ocean / breeze	bread / b_tter
leaf / tree	music / l_rics
sweet / sour	sh_e / sock
movie / actress	phone / bo_k
gasoline / engine	chi_s / salsa
high school / college	penc_l / paper
turkey / stuffing	river / b_at
fruit / vegetable	be_r / wine
computer / chip	tel_vision / radio
chair / couch	l_nch / dinner

Now, turn the page over and, without looking, try to recall as many of the word pairs as you can. Which column do you remember most from?

I've tried this in live audiences many times and, of course, Daniel Coyle has extensively tested it too. Almost without exception, people remember far more from column B – the one you had to work harder to read and process.

That's the first principle of practice: make it hard; make it difficult.

So why is this?

It's to do with neural pathways and a substance called myelin. Myelin is the substance that covers the neural pathways that take the messages between neurones. So what you have in your brain is a circuit of nerve fibres that are 'insulated' by myelin. The more myelin, or insulation, that wraps these pathways, the faster the signal can travel and the more automatically and easily you can perform a task. Every movement you make requires a neural signal to fire off across the brain. If I decide to reach over and pick up my tasty beverage, a certain set of well-worn signals will fire off in my brain. And it'll be so automatic that I won't even think about it. Those pathways have a thick layer of myelin, which I started laying down many years ago when my parents decided it was time to move on from the Tommy Tippee mug and get my manual dexterity to a level that I could hold a cup without a lid.

If I decide to buy a new keyboard for my computer with a slightly different layout, then I'm going to have to do some myelin laying in an effort to get as fast as I was on my old one. But, as we all know, sometimes we can't be bothered to adopt new tools or tasks. We give up and go back to the old keyboard and make excuses about the new one being rubbish.

For any new process, your brain fires all these signals down all sorts of pathways to begin with. It doesn't really know the fastest way, so it's inefficient. And the signal going through is like an old whistling 28.8 modem. But with time, and repeated performing of the task, you gradually up the speed of these connections until you have broadband. Tiger Woods has mega-fast super-duper broadband in his brain for golf tasks.

This means that you have to practise; that you have to take that new activity and build a lot of myelin. If you have a flaw in your swing, you have to lay down a lot of myelin over a set of new neural pathways before you can get it right. The peculiar thing about myelin is that harder practice means that you make more of it and learn faster. That's why it was easier to remember the list of harder words in column B.

To get real results, we need to practise hard to accelerate the speed at which myelin is laid. You can take a new swing and go to the range and simply hit fifty balls as best you can, but that isn't going to make much difference. What you need to do is set conditions so that every ball hit in practice has a measurable outcome. You must do things on the range that are really hard. Out on the course I use my lovely easy-to-hit Mizuno irons; on the range I have a lethal two-iron blade. On the course I use a lovely, large-headed driver; on the range I often use an old MacGregor persimmon wood. Often I won't allow myself to leave the range until I've put a certain number of balls into the fifty-yard nets, or hit ten balls in a row between two targets in the distance. I'll often make up arbitrary little games in which I have to hit twenty 'perfect' strikes in a row with a certain club. It'll not surprise you that a key part of Gary Player's bunker practice involved him not allowing himself to leave the practice area until he'd holed a certain number of bunker shots.

 JOHN'S TRUE STORIES

One evening, long before I'd started my research into learning and neuroscience, I was standing at the range and decided I wanted to get better at chipping. I was always a fan of pitching, even from very close range, but knew that a chip-and-run style of shot would be more effective on links courses.

So I set myself a task. I pitched a ball fifteen feet or so out in front of me and tried to hit it. I figured that this would be a good way to get better and keep focused. I reckoned I'd hit it within about fifteen shots or so. After about thirty shots I started to get frustrated. I still hadn't hit it but had come close several times so decided to put real pressure on myself. I wasn't to leave the range until I hit the ball. One hundred and seventy-eight balls later, long after the range had closed and almost crying with frustration, I finally hit the ball.

No matter how frustrated I got and how cross with myself I became, I knew I had no option but to keep chipping better and better in order to get home to my bed. So I gradually forced myself to chip well and put my neural pathways under a huge amount of load.

When I next ventured out onto the golf course the effect the practice had had on my chipping was almost magical. I felt much more control and was much better at getting the ball close to the hole.

Don't fall into the trap of taking advice from mediocre players. Make sure that you grasp how practice works, and only take advice from people who have actually achieved the results you're striving for.

. . . .

10. Create a cast iron pre-shot routine

You can tell a good golfer from a bad golfer from a long way away by watching their pre-shot routine.

It's vital to craft a pre-shot routine that sets you up for success. A pre-shot routine should allow you to go through a visualisation process and clearly see where the ball should go. It should allow you to be comfortable with your club choice and confident that swing thoughts or fear of hazards won't dominate your swing.

By the time you address the ball your thought process should be finished. Touring pros, for example, take little practice swings and perhaps make a final check on something they've been working on. And then they step forward and pull the trigger.

That's what you need to do. You do not need to stand over the ball and produce a few practice swings, none of which will look anything like what you actually produce. You need to do all this well behind the ball and then, with a crystal-clear picture in your mind of what will happen, you should stride forward and hit it.

An ideal set-up is as follows:

1. Stand beside your bag and take all factors into consideration. How strong is the wind? What hazards are in the way? What is the safest part of the fairway to hit to?

2. Choose your club based on these factors and

then stand a couple of yards behind the ball. If you are working on any particular aspect of your swing, then take a couple of small swings to ensure you have the correct feeling.

3. Use the club to point down the fairway to a very specific target. Start to visualise the ball going off the face of your club towards that target.

4. Focusing on the target, move forward and address the ball.

5. As you're addressing the ball, keep fluid and think about nothing but the target.

6. Strike the ball.

 JOHN'S TRUE STORIES

One day I watched a large group of golfers tee off for a society match at Blackwood. Most were poor golfers and almost all followed the same pre-shot routine: they took a couple of nervous practice swings and addressed the ball. Often they would check their grip or some other specific aspect of their stance and then they'd wait, starting a huge battle of wills with the ball, making very sure that by the time they actually hit the thing they had truly showed it who was boss. The trigger seemed to be not when they were ready, but when they felt they had intimidated the ball sufficiently. At this point they'd flail wildly at it and, of course, the ball would show the golfer who was boss by sailing merrily into the trees.

The pre-shot routines varied a little from hacker to hacker, but were broadly similar. Then a few low handicappers came along, and watching them was a totally different experience. I could tell their play was all target based and they were visualising the shot in some form. Then they took a couple of fluid practice swings, paused, looked at the target and pulled the trigger. Watching a golf tournament on television will show you exactly the same thing.

. . . .

11. The left-handed pitching technique

There was one tip that I discovered during my challenge that made the most substantial difference to my game and remains at the very centre of all my practice. Nothing improved my short game more, and nothing can help me get my full swing back on track as quickly as the left-handed pitching technique.

My discovery of this technique came about as a result of two factors: pain in my right wrist and an old John Daly DVD … In the early days of my challenge I practised too often and too hard off the range mats at my local course. I started to get a lot of pain in my right wrist and was given a telling-off by the local pro, Debbie Hanna. Debbie showed me the post-surgery scars on her right wrist and explained that she'd been out of action for nine months as a result of over-practice at the very peak of her career as a tour professional. Debbie advised that I should completely rest my wrist for a couple of weeks and focus on putting. But nobody likes putting practice …

The problem was that the golf bug had bitten me. I'd seen some progress and I had an obsessive desire to keep improving. I decided to visit the range, hide from Debbie and attempt some practice with my right hand gently guiding the club – but not gripping it with any strength.

This caused me to slow down and focus on tempo

rather than distance. With a little more experimentation, I worked out that I could hit the ball with my left hand only. I was forced to keep my body very still – which was a bonus as I had a problem with too much body movement in my swing at that stage – and those two weeks of right wrist rest produced a leap forward in my basic swing technique.

During these two weeks I also bought an old DVD on eBay for £1, called *A Round with John Daly*. This was one of a series of videos in which the golfer discussed their career and shared a few of their personal tips. In the DVD, John demonstrated his practice technique around the green. He used his lob wedge to strike some absolutely beautiful pitches to within inches of the hole … using his left hand only. And he explained how important this was to his short game practice.

On YouTube, I then found a video of John conducting a clinic. Again he was demonstrating the technique and hitting beautiful full wedges with his left arm only.

Throughout the rest of my challenge year, I stuck with this technique and it made a tremendous impact on my skills around the green. To try it for yourself, follow this routine:

- Hit ten wedge shots at the practice range with both hands to a very specific target. Ideally you want to hit the ball between two markers so you can give yourself a score out of ten.

- Next hit ten shots with your left arm only. Don't worry about how well you're striking the ball – just attempt to hit it as well as you can. Record your score.

- Finally, hit another ten shots with both hands. The minute you put your right hand back on the club again you'll have an almost magical feeling of control.

I've tested this process in clinics with thousands of golfers and nobody has ever scored worse in the second scoring session than they did in the first.

Not long after I finished the challenge I was asked by a golfing journalist to record a few videos of the practices that had made the biggest difference to my game. The 'John Daly left-handed pitching technique' had more than 35,000 views within ten days – by far the most popular of the videos we shot.

12. The Clock Face, or 3 x 4 technique

This is a technique that takes very little time to perfect, but is incredibly powerful, not just in terms of your confidence levels in tricky situations, but also in terms of your scoring. After I started using this system, analysis of my scores showed it had saved me between three and five strokes per round.

To use this technique, think of your hands as being like the hands of a clock face so that you can produce swings with the left hand at 7.30, 9.00 and 10.30:

7.30 *Here your left hand is 45° to the ground and 45° to the parallel.*

9.00 *Here your left hand is parallel to the ground.*

Then apply these three different swings to your four (or however many you have) different wedges. I used my standard Mizuno pitching wedge, which was about 46 degrees and then (after endless trial and error) ended up with Ping Tour wedges at 52, 56 and 60 degrees.

The system does take a while to set up, and it requires

10.30 *45° above the parallel.*

a little dedication to calculate your distances, but the result is a grid of twelve different distances that you can replicate under pressure.

To calculate your distances, hit ten balls with each wedge at each distance. Make a note of these distances and then repeat the process regularly over a period of about four or five sessions. Ideally you shouldn't allow yourself to see the previous results so there's less risk of you trying to replicate a previous session's distances

You should aim to hit each shot with roughly the same type of swing. The only thing to change is the length of the backswing, which obviously increases the speed with which you hit the ball. There is a school of thought that says your follow-through should only be as long as your backswing, but I tend to go a little past this. At the end, review your distances, and if there are any major discrepancies, go out and test those distances until you have a figure you are comfortable with. You must be comfortable with them, since you need to be able to rely on these in pressurised situations. It's a great confidence boost to know that you have 67 yards to the pin and can simply dial in a 9.00 sand wedge, or have the option of a 9.00 pitching wedge or a full 10.30 sand wedge for an approach of a little over 90 yards.

If you only have three wedges don't worry – just work it out for three. But I can heartily recommend going the full four-wedge route to get full flexibility.

For your interest, my distances are as follows:

	Pitching Wedge	Gap Wedge	Sand Wedge	Lob Wedge
7.30	70	55	40	25
9.00	95	82	67	50
10.30	125	110	92	75

13. The driver as an eight iron

One of the simplest tricks I developed during my challenge was to imagine that I was striking with an eight iron (the club I find it easiest to strike with). I looked down and was able to make the club head morph into an eight-iron shape. I gripped down a little so that the club felt a little more like an eight, and struck it at about the same tempo as if I was in my perfect eight-iron distance.

It's a remarkably powerful process. I'm a fan of the principle that a driver swing is different to an iron swing, but only when you're really striking the ball well. If I'm honest, I probably imagine my driver as an eight iron nearly 50 per cent of the time. It means I might lose a little distance off the tee, and can look slightly unorthodox, but most people don't notice – and I'll strike the ball further than I would have with the three wood (although the same principle applies to that club too).

The number one priority is to have confidence standing over the ball and to feel in control – even if your game isn't quite where you wish it was, or if external factors are distracting you.

Swing the long irons as though they all have a no. 7 stamped on the sole. If you swing the 3-iron like you do the 7-iron, you won't swing too hard or try to help the ball in the air – which is the tendency with the long irons.

JACK NICKLAUS

14. Creating the perfect golf swing

The pursuit of the perfect golf swing is a huge reason why Ben Hogan remains such a compelling character, to me and millions of golfers throughout the world. His seminal book, *Five Lessons – The Modern Fundamentals of Golf*, still sits at or near the top of the golf charts on an almost continual basis.

Beyond that though, there is always the underlying suspicion that Hogan had found the 'secret': that he had met that little guru at the top of the mythical mountain, and in a few whispered words, the secret had been bestowed upon him. In our feverish little golf minds, Hogan had then climbed down the mountain and chosen to apply his new-found knowledge to his own game, rather than share it with the rest of us.

That, of course, is nonsense. People talk about his wrist cupping or 'supination' as if that's the answer or the secret, but clearly this isn't the case. A golf swing is a combination of so many factors that one simple wrist position can never hope to be close to being the perfect answer.

I learnt most about how to improve my swing from Jim McLellan. Jim had witnessed the likes of Sam Snead and Ben Hogan first-hand, and was the inspirational golf teacher that I discovered early in my challenge. I bought Jim's video course and then sent him videos of my swing during the year. Jim's teachings are a little different from the norm but very powerful. This is what he taught me:

1. Keep it simple. Stop thinking about endless positions and angles at each stage.

2. Keep your hands high at the top of the backswing and the same at follow-through.

3. Keep your head still.

4. Concentrate on practising without hitting a ball, in front of a mirror, and keep comparing your swing to a perfect swing (or to the best that you can find – and Jim's is as good as you might expect).

Legendary golf coach John Jacobs also regarded golf as 'two turns and a swish'.

With that said, it's vital that you get yourself into the correct position to begin with. Your grip, alignment, stance and ball position should all be perfect. If you can get these fundamentals right, the swing shouldn't be too hard.

So, here's exactly how I created my golf swing …

I downloaded the video of Jim's swing and then spent hours and hours and hours (and then a few more) watching it and deeply, intensely imagining that it was me swinging, not Jim. I spent time learning a neuro-linguistic programming (NLP) process called modelling and used it to help me picture myself, in great detail, swinging the club as Jim would swing it. I visualised that I actually *was* Jim. I heard the trees rustling, felt the breeze and sensed the weight of his hat on my head. I had the video on my phone, on a loop on my computer and edited a version which ran at lower speed. I played Jim's swing at every opportunity.

And then I stood in my back garden and swung the club as much as I could in EXACTLY the way Jim did. I then recorded my swing to see how similar it was to Jim's. What I didn't do, however, was analyse the position of my hands or treat my swing like an engineering exercise. That would always muddle my mind.

So, in a nutshell, to improve your swing you need to:

1. Get your fundamentals right in terms of grip, stance, alignment and ball position.

2. Watch a 'perfect swing' a LOT.

3. Swing in the style of that perfect swing and compare via video recording.

4. Take it to the course …

15. The Harvey Penick grip tip (and a couple of others)

He (Harvey Penick) started by modifying my grip, which he thought was the foundation for everything. He emphasised placing my hands on the club as opposed to twisting them into place. He told me to practise placing my hands on the club and that's pretty much all I did from 8 a.m. to 5 p.m. He told me to do it at home until it became second nature. He said two things that really stuck with me. One was, 'If you have a good grip, it will be easier to make a good swing than a bad one.' The other was, 'If you have a bad grip, you don't want a good swing.' After I got that grip down pat, I started getting real good, real fast.

KATHY WHITWORTH, 6 majors, 88 LPGA Tour wins

Of all the slightly boring fundamentals that you must work on, the grip is perhaps the most important to master. And also one of the most difficult …

I still remember – in vivid detail because she was so cross – my golf pro becoming exasperated with me eight months into my *Dream On* challenge for not having mastered how to grip a golf club. If you don't have a good golf club grip, you are going to find it extremely difficult to hit the ball in a consistent and accurate manner. If you are a single degree out in terms of the position of the club head at the point of impact with the ball, you'll experience about 15 yards of dispersion.

There are lots of ways to learn a decent golf grip, but

perhaps the easiest is the the tip from Harvey Penick, the legendary coach who taught Ben Crenshaw, Tom Kite and Kathy Whitworth, amongst others.

Grip Tip number one

Harvey Penick's yard rule concept. If you grip a yard rule, or indeed any simple ruler, you're almost forced into a perfect golf club grip. It's a simple and effective way to feel what a grip should be naturally, rather than getting too caught up in the mechanics.

Grip Tip number two

Study Ben Hogan's grip in his classic *Five Lessons* book, and compare it to yours. This was the picture of the grip I had stuck to the cork board beside my desk. Rather than getting caught up in the mechanics of how I should be gripping the club, I found it far easier to simply grip and compare.

Grip Tip number three

Purchase two pre-formed grips and put one on a club that you use for practice. It's generally very easy to buy a used six iron which matches your set, and you can put the grip on this. You can't use it for play on the course but, when you're practising, you can be assured that your grip is being forced into the correct position. The second pre-formed grip should be left as is and you can simply hold it in your hands while you watch television or at any other opportunity.

Grip Tip number four

The final way to learn how to grip a golf club and integrate a good grip into your game is to practise at the range. Over a few range sessions simply tweak and adjust your grip so you can learn what different grips mean in terms of your ability to shape or hit the ball consistently. Make sure you don't just tweak the angles at which your hands are on the club, but also make changes to how much your fingers and thumbs are in contact with the grip itself.

By doing this you'll learn exactly what works for you rather than what 'should' work. By using a grip that you know works for you, you will radically improve your confidence when out on the course. And that, as ever, remains the fundamental key to shooting great scores.

16. Alignment and setup are critical

Even if you perfect your grip, incorrect alignment in the rest of your swing will cause you almost as many problems as a bad swing. Very few golfers would argue with this, but – if you look closely at most of the golfers at a driving range – it's a point of view to which about 90 per cent only pay lip service.

Watch a line of touring professionals at the range and you'll see that most of them focus a great deal on their alignment and core fundamentals. They have a variety of devices to help them check that their practices are effective. Watch a line of amateur golfers at your local range and you might see a few with a club lined up with their feet but in most cases this is really just to look cool and they're paying very little attention to it.

In *Golf My Way*, Jack Nicklaus describes setup as being 90 per cent of good shot making. Greg Norman's Tip #20 on his Shark.com website also emphasises its importance:

> Alignment is my No. 1 priority when I begin to
> play a golf shot. And because accurate alignment is
> a demanding and sometimes elusive quality, I try
> to simplify the aiming process as much as possible.
> I focus everything on my clubface.
>
> Once I've decided upon the type of shot I want
> to play, the first move I make is to set my club

position behind the ball, so that it's facing squarely at the target. Holding the club in my right hand only, I approach the ball from behind, sighting up and down that imaginary line that extends from the ball to my target. I then assume a wide-open stance, half facing the target, still tracking that line from the target to the ball. At this point, I set my club down behind the ball and swivel the clubface minutely back and forth until it's in exact position, facing dead at the target. Only after this is set do I proceed with the other elements of the grip and address.

Once you have your clubface sorted, you need to address your stance. The classic mode of checking that your feet are aligned with the hole is a little flawed. If you watch a line of golfers you'll see that, even with their feet aligned, their knees and hips can often be way out. So focus at least as much on getting these straight too.

I slightly open my left foot at address, so I judge my stance by looking at my knees and hips. This allows me a feeling of getting through the ball and avoiding my natural flaw – the 'out-to-in' swing – and, in addition, Ben Hogan did the same thing so it allows me to feel a sense of connection to him. Which, from my point of view, can only ever be a good thing

I adopt a square stance for all shots of fifty yards and further. In this range I'm using a mostly full or three-quarter swing and I want to be consistently mechanical in actions. From fifty yards and in I play in a different way. I'm thinking about the game and my shot in a much more creative way and will therefore open my stance a little and remove the classic images of perfect alignment from my brain.

You can't be scared standing on the first tee. You've got to learn to deal with that. I had a system. I made my mind go back to the most basic fundamentals of the game: my grip, my stance, the position of my head, the very first things I learned. It became a habit. If you watch old videos of me getting ready to play, you'll see me gripping and regripping the club, waggling, taking my stance, and then standing normally. I'm reviewing the fundamentals. It made me think of what I should be doing, as opposed to how important it was. I highly recommend it.

ARNOLD PALMER

17. The importance of balance

If you go back to the basics and assume that nothing good can come out of a horrible follow-through (and it can't), then try to visualise a beautiful balanced follow-through as your last swing-thought before you hit the ball. I use an image of Retief Goosen's follow-through from the *Golf Digest* site and sometimes also hold an image of Tiger's follow-through. Tiger talks about wanting his belt buckle to point to the target. So just before I strike the ball, I create a picture in my mind in which I am standing perfectly balanced with my hands high and my belt buckle pointing at the target.

During the challenge I also got a chance to study Rory McIlroy's follow-through. Even in those days, when he was in his mid-teens, Rory had an explosive swing. I watched him at the range for many hours over that year and saw a very noticeable slowing down of the club towards the end of the backswing. I saw this characteristic first in the practice of some of his junior contemporaries. This technique forces an exceptionally well-balanced finish. On a spectacularly big hit Rory never falls off or has any loss of control. Luke Donald may not produce the same explosive power as Rory and has a slightly less conventional follow-through, but he's another superb ambassador for this technique. I subsequently mentioned to my mentor Jim McLellan that I'd observed an almost identical deliberate 'slow down' on his follow-through. It was so instinctive for him, though, that he hadn't even noticed he did it.

The key thing is to finish in balance. And if you're struggling, take a balanced follow-through as your only aim for a round and see the positive effect it has on your scores.

Sean Foley says that the greatest tip he ever received was to 'do nothing at the expense of great balance'. He advises addressing the ball as normal and then pulling your right foot (assuming you're right-handed) back about twelve inches so that you're standing on your toe. Now strike a bucket of balls using your right leg only as a very mild stabiliser. This is an exceptional way of swinging in control and teaching yourself the importance of a balanced swing.

18. Practise your bunker shots

During my challenge I had been playing my bunker shots very badly and reached an 'enough!' state of mind. Conveniently, Blackwood had a practice bunker area at the end of the range so I decided to go up with my sand wedge and devote two hours of practice to getting better.

I bought a couple of buckets of balls, scattered them around the bunker and spent the time getting better. No great secrets. No magic tips or epiphanies. I just committed to each shot and played around with hard and soft surfaces and the distance I hit behind the ball.

The next day I played a round of golf with my father. I ended up in a tough bunker, with no ability to see the flag, let alone the hole, which was several metres above. I laughed at the baptism of fire my new bunker technique was getting, but tried my best to focus on what I'd learnt, and swung the club. The ball went into the hole. It was one of the most incredible examples of how a little work can make a huge difference. I can't claim that I became the new Gary Player or Ernie Els after that but the practice made a lasting and quantifiable improvement to my bunker play, which continues to stand me in good stead.

Another trick I learnt, this time from Gary Player, was to chip and pitch some balls along the beach. You cannot fail to get better at sand play with this technique and it falls into the powerful 'play practice' category outlined in Tip 49.

Many golfers don't take time to practise in bunkers – the practice bunker at Blackwood is so underused that grass regularly grows in it; but people regularly queue at the range to practise their driving. A classic example of 80/20 being applied the wrong way.

Would you like to know the fastest way to take several strokes off your game? Spend two hours in a bunker. Two hours is all it takes to raise yourself out of the fear-and-doubt group (about 90 per cent of all golfers) to the point where you can play from sand with confidence.

In truth, bunker play isn't that difficult. As Walter Hagen said, it's the only shot where you don't have to hit the ball. But the best way to learn is to teach yourself, by experimenting with varying ball positions, degrees of openness in your clubface and shaft, and lengths and paces of swing. Each combination of these elements moves the sand – and thus your ball – in a different way. In the course of a two-hour session you'll arrive at an understanding of this bunker-play physics, and in the process you'll discover how to play several different shots.

GREG NORMAN, Sharkwatch www.shark.com

19. Err on the side of thin (think Sweep not Punch)

Much of my practice, and probably yours, will happen on hard range mats. Whilst this allows us to be able to practise all year, under cover, the mats are bad for your game and body in many ways. I damaged my wrist so badly on these mats that I had to have surgery to fix it last year and will probably need further operations in the future. They also are far too forgiving – you can bash away with very little sense of how crisply you're hitting the ball.

If I've spent a lot of time at the range I have a tendency to hit the ball a little fat when I'm out on the course. To cure this I hit a succession of balls from a wooden board that I sometimes carried with me, using a couple of old clubs. This practice can damage the clubs but is extremely effective in forcing me to focus on a beautiful clean contact. Given the problems that I have with my wrist, this may seem a bizarre thing to do, but try it: you'll be surprised at how easy it is to pick the ball up with no jarring action at all. Range mats will always cause me more problems than wood.

Another solution is to hit from paths near ranges, or visit a range that has poor outdoor surfaces. Nothing sharpens your iron play faster than trying to hit balls off poor surfaces. When you get back to the course, the fairway will appear like the opening day of the Masters at Augusta and your ability to strike in a sweeping manner will greatly improve.

History tells us that Harry Vardon was a wonderful long iron player, and also that he rarely took a divot with any club. The two go together, in my view. Many golfers would immeasurably improve their long-iron play, and lose the fear of those valuable clubs, if they would think of sweeping – rather than punching or scooping – the clubhead through the ball.

JACK NICKLAUS

20. Practise with distractions

One of my greatest joys during my challenge year was the almost Zen-like state that I achieved through solitary practice. According to Sam Snead, I am blessed with a fundamental disadvantage when it comes to getting good at golf: 'People who talk really fast or dart around generally have a hard time playing golf.' Sadly, he's describing me to a T! I have always struggled to keep still, stay quiet, and resist darting off to try out new ideas or concepts. So the golf challenge was about teaching myself some mental discipline and ways to quieten my mind. And it worked: I was able to practise for hours, often in the howling wind and rain, and summon up an inner Ben Hogan to keep me focused.

And undoubtedly this solitary practice helped my golf and helped me to groove my swing changes into place. But there is also a flaw in this method: practising alone, at the far end of a practice range, under cover and in darkness, bears very little relationship to a round on a golf course. The complete lack of distractions may be very good for my focus, but doesn't help with the sort of mental toughness needed on the course.

Earl Woods famously made noises and distracted Tiger when he was practising on the range – not as a consequence of a bad shot from Tiger, but during the shot. And, as with everything Earl did, it was part of a conscious effort to help Tiger to improve. He knew that Tiger was going to encounter endless distractions on the course and he wanted to make these pale in comparison to what Tiger had to endure at the range. It's hard to argue with the results. Tiger remains the most focused golfer out there – in good times or bad. So, as ever, success leaves clues.

> If a cell phone or camera going off disrupts you, you've got issues with concentration on your golf game. If you're totally absorbed in the shot you're playing, how can you hear anything?
>
> JACK NICKLAUS

So, with this in mind, I would haul my sorry little backside up to the noisiest part of the range. I'd position myself right by the guys who were out for a bit of craic before they went into the bar. I didn't have an Earl Woods to shout at me, and don't naturally have Jack or Ben's astonishing focus. So I made the very best of what I had. And I'd force myself not to be distracted by the Happy Gilmores and all their shouting, laughing and horrific over-the-top swings.

And now, when I'm out on the course, I find it vastly easier to not be distracted by shouts in the distance or playing partners shifting in and out of my view.

21. The secrets of distance

It took a lot of work, both in the gym and on my swing, to be able to hit the ball a long way consistently. Being a red-blooded male in my late thirties, I still saw this part of the game as a critical part of 'man golf'. Whatever you think about that, there's no doubt that hitting the ball a long way helps enormously with your scores. On a 6,300-yard course (like Blackwood), if you can hit 300-yard shots, you will be hitting wedges into the greens on par fours. And since my wedge play and short game was the only area in which I truly excelled, you can see how it became simply a matter of time until I broke par.

So what did I learn in terms of the keys to distance? There are lots of little factors that can help your distance, but there are two key practices that enable you to hit the ball a long way.

1. Make a proper full turn with your shoulders, firmly braced against a strong right leg (or left if you're a lefty). Golf instruction is awash with suggestions for horrible arms-only swings for out-of-shape golfers when, in fact, there are techniques and stretches that can add enormous increases in shoulder-turn performance for no effort. So don't think that just because you're getting a little older and stiffer you need to adopt some sort of different 'easy' swing and give up on the joy of a proper swing with a proper shoulder

turn. If you work at this, you'll add twenty yards to your drives within a week.

2. Accept that the driver swing, certainly in terms of distance shots, is a different swing to an iron swing. And that means staying behind the ball. National Long Drive champion Sean Fister suggests you swing your driver as if it's a ball that you're skimming across the water, or a bat hitting a baseball. You must have that feeling of being behind the ball at impact. Not so far that you fall back, but exactly the same position as if you were skimming a ball a long way.

Practise these two drills with some slow motion swings in which you take the club back and ensure that your left shoulder has turned past the ball within your line of sight: i.e. you're looking down at the ball with your shoulder on your right-hand side. If you can do this, you're well on the way to ensuring that you have enough shoulder turn.

Now return the club back to an impact position where you feel you have the most power, i.e. with your body slightly behind the ball. Work on these two positions at the range, or even in your back garden, and the next time you hit a drive you'll see a substantial increase in distance.

22. Incline the right knee

I have a natural tendency to straighten my right leg on the backswing which prevents a lot of power from being stored as you coil. Ben Hogan and Jack Nicklaus both advocate a slight incline or 'setting-in' of the right knee. This allows you to feel a tension and gives something to coil against whilst taking your arms back. It creates a feeling of power coming from the body and not the hands or arms, which is where the real distance will come from.

The trick is to set and keep your weight on the inside of the right foot. If your weight moves over to the outside of the foot, the knee is bound either to stiffen or buckle outward.

To help you learn the correct 'feel' stick a golf ball under the outside part of your right instep on the practice tee. It will cant the foot and the knee inward, and you'll learn what it really feels like to 'coil the spring' on the backswing.

JACK NICKLAUS

23. Create a 'bubble'

Creating a bubble is invaluable when you are playing with partners or in situations where there are lots of outside influences, such as when your partner is having a bad day and is ranting and raving about his game and going in for club-throwing histrionics. It's hard not to empathise – and it's also hard not to say the wrong thing. Likewise, if you're playing a match and your opponent is using a few unpleasant gamesmanship techniques, you can easily lose your focus. Many people struggle badly with first tee nerves, and knowing that there are people gathered around waiting to play can be extremely off-putting.

All of these situations can be alleviated by the bubble. The minute you feel any negative outside influences, try to imagine a there's a huge bubble covering you. I like to visualise a sort of whooshing noise as the bubble covers me. My bubble totally isolates me from the outside world so that the only things with me are the positive golfing experiences I've had in the past. I quickly run through a few past successes, with the specifics varying depending on the shot I'm going to play. So if it's a putt, then I just think of previous great ones I've made, and, if it's a drive, I imagine a previous time where I split the fairway with my driver.

This reverses any negativity that I may have been experiencing, and allows me to reboot my normal positive self. When I've hit the shot, I allow the bubble to disappear – or maybe I'll keep it but allow some outside influences to filter through. This tip is all thanks to David Walters, who I introduced in Tip 8.

24. Focusing on your target – the hole

Bob Rotella tells a story about working with Hal Sutton. Sutton had been the 'next big thing' for a while, but his scores had started to drop off, and much of his downward slide could be attributed to his putting. Rotella persuaded him to practise by not looking at the ball when he hit it, focusing only on the target – the hole. Sutton tried this for several hours and quickly noticed an improvement. So he took it out onto the course at the tournament in which he was playing and shot a staggering 63 – the course record.

I tried this myself and found it to be a brilliant way of not getting caught up in the mechanics of the stroke. You don't have to take it out onto the course, but as an exercise to emphasise the importance of the target, and to remind you how little you need to focus on mechanics, it is absolutely invaluable. And the results are particularly impressive on long putts.

Similarly, Earl Woods taught the young Tiger to roll balls to the hole with his eyes closed, focusing entirely on an image of the ball falling into the hole. This target-based imaging is absolutely vital.

25. Swing with your feet together

Stand at a practice range and watch a bunch of amateur golfers hitting balls. Then, if you can, watch a group of professionals practising on a range at a tournament. There will be many differences between the two groups but none more obvious or startling than the difference in balance between the pros and the amateurs. Without exception pro golfers, especially at the range, swing completely in balance. And the majority of amateur golfers finish their swing slightly (or enormously) off balance.

To play better golf we must play in balance. And the simplest way to do that is to practise hitting balls with your feet together. This is a tip so old I remember it from my brief period playing as child when we were taught by Bob Cockcroft at Ballyreagh – just down the road from the magnificent links course at Royal Portrush. It's a very simple process. Simply hit a lot of balls, as well as you can, with your feet together. To make it even harder and increase your balance even further, you can cross your feet, one over the other.

Sometimes these simple tips can have almost magical powers. Jack Nicklaus recommends this one as a way to improve your tempo, and David Leadbetter suggests it as a cure for your slice.

Fifty shots hit like this could do wonders for your tempo and rhythm. This manoeuvre is also a fine way to start developing a tempo slower than the one you've been playing with.

JACK NICKLAUS

26. Understand and focus on the impact position

Ultimately that's what everything else boils down to. Everything that goes on in your head, on your backswing and on the follow-through is all about one thing – ensuring that you get into a perfect impact position and strike the ball well. But few amateur golfers have a crystal-clear notion in their heads as to what exactly this position should be.

To ensure you get a clean ball strike you must not only understand this position, but keep drilling and practising it. If you can keep it foremost in your mind it's much easier to build a good swing. In essence there are just five elements that differentiate it from your address position.

1. The shaft of your club will be leaning slightly forward and your hands will be ahead of where they were at address.

2. Your weight will have shifted onto your leading leg (left leg for right-handed golfers).

3. Your hips will have rotated a little – but no more than 45 degrees.

4. Your shoulders will have rotated a little but will not have rotated as much as your hips.

5. Your right foot (for right-handed golfers) will

have shifted weight onto the inside and your heel will have started to rise.

Getting in this position allows you to strike the ball first and hit down hard and through the ball with the lowest part of the swing after you strike it.

The understanding of this process is something that can be worked on well away from the course. All you need are some examples of great impact positions (available with the free videos that accompany this book) and a full-length mirror. Practise getting that feeling of being in the correct position at home and then take it to the range.

One way to drill this position into your game is to simply hit some balls by addressing the ball in your impact position. It's a little odd at first, and I would advise just using a three-quarter swing, but it very quickly illustrates how you should be striking the ball.

I like to put a tee into the end of my club and then hit a lot of fifty-yard pitches ensuring that the tee is pointed well to the left of my belt buckle at impact. If I focus on that one simple metric all the other five points fall into place. This is a drill I use a lot because I have a tendency to reach an impact position not quite forward enough.

Modern smartphones and cameras have the ability to shoot very fast video with multiple frames per second. If you can get hold of one of these you should be recording your swing and comparing your impact position with that of a professional and in relation to the five points above. You'll almost certainly find that it's not exactly where you thought it was and that's a good thing! It allows you to diagnose your own problems and worry less about where you are on the backswing or follow-through and focus all your efforts on the impact.

Think about the shaft, not the ball

This can be a difficult concept for amateurs to grasp, but if you want to use the club properly and hit the ball flush, the bottom of your swing has to be in front of the ball. Your shaft should be leaning toward the target at impact, and the divot should start after you strike the ball. But if you're focusing too hard on hitting the ball, your wrists can break down as you try to scoop it into the air.

SEAN FOLEY, *Golf Digest*

27. Trick your mind with mental imagery

When I was young, I played most of my golf with my older brother. One day he was having a particularly 'hot' day with the putter. Intrigued by what he was doing, and frustrated by the margin by which he was beating me, I asked how he was putting so well.

He explained that he was imagining a clear groove in the grass that ran directly from the ball to the hole. After he had read the putt properly all he needed to do was confidently set the ball on its way along this groove. As long as he struck the ball at the right speed, the groove would do the rest. We both used this method and holed some huge putts – it seemed like magic.

This technique still helps with my confidence when it comes to longer putts and many other aspects of my game. In so many cases, we tend to think about avoiding bunkers, water, trees, railway tracks, and so on. And we all know how much of a problem those thoughts create – we tend to hit the ball straight into the hazard that we keep telling ourselves to avoid. Psychologists tell us that the mind can't understand negative commands. In other words if we think 'Don't hit it into the water', our dopey little brains hear 'hit it into the water'. And so we do.

Equally the brain often cannot tell what is real or not. If we watch a really good movie on a big screen, for example, we can become so completely absorbed in what's going on that we forget that we're sitting in a cinema with sticky crumbs of popcorn stuck to the front of our shirt. We're actually inside the movie, right in the middle of the action.

The legendary Jackie Burke, winner of two majors, used to trick his mind to his advantage:

When I look down the fairway from the tee and want to play a fade, I see a huge wall on the left side of the fairway. I see a jai-alai court, where the ball will bounce off the wall and back into play if I miss the fairway. That gives me mental freedom and the ability to swing with a bit of recklessness, which is necessary to be a good driver of the ball. Take that wall down, and you get tense and start steering the ball short and crooked. Let it go, man! Freewheel it!

When I was having trouble putting, Raymond told me to imagine the ball was a small locomotive on a track that led straight to the hole. 'Now, Arnold,' he said, 'you really have to believe it's a train. Those of us who do believe can smell the smoke.' It's a lesson I've called on many times since.

ARNOLD PALMER, from his foreword to
The Elements of Scoring by Ray Floyd

28. 'Throw the seeds' at the top of your backswing

High handicappers often flip their wrists at the point that their club makes contact with the ball. To fix this, Jackie Burke advises that you should imagine your right hand is filled with seeds when you're at the top of your backswing and that you want to spread those seeds over as wide an area as you can. You'll discover that you can only disperse the seeds properly if you maintain an angle in your right wrist. Try it now as you sit and read this. You can't throw the seeds over a long distance if you flip your wrist – if you do that, the seeds will go up and over your face or land at your feet. Jackie believes strongly in still being able to aggressively throw the club into the ball with your right hand, but says you'll only get power and accuracy if you release the club as if you were sowing those seeds.

This is a great mental image. Whatever you do, though, make sure that you remove any form of flipping action completely from your swing. The club face has plenty of loft to get the ball up in the air – it doesn't need any help from you.

JOHN'S TRUE STORIES

Approximately halfway through my challenge, I spent some time on the Old Course at Portstewart. This is the course that

I played during my teenage years and it has a very special place in my heart. At 4,783 yards and a par 64, it's not exactly the toughest test in golf, but the first few holes, stretching along classic North Antrim coastline, are a joy.

I played the first sixteen holes with mixed results and sat down on the edge of the road with my notebook to record where I was with my golf. I noticed a four ball playing up to the tricky second green and observed their balls miss the hole and trickle down into the little valley around the front edge of the hole. All four of them then pulled out their wedges and attempted to get the ball back up and near the hole.

And all four of them did the classic high handicapper flipping motion, attempting to scoop the ball to safety with the inevitably woeful results. To continue conforming to the classic high handicapper cliché, they then all stared down at the face of their club as if the club was at fault and not their action.

I sat for another half hour and watched the next two groups play through. Without exception, those golfers who missed the green did the flip. And, also without exception, the results weren't good. My (possibly arrogant) assumption is that not one of these players ever spent time trying to get rid of this flipping motion.

. . . .

29. Protect your back and avoid those horrible up and down arm swings

Golf is a game of pride as much as anything else. It's a beautiful, fluid, athletic sport. There's absolutely no need to give up and adopt one of those 'arms-only' swings. The internet is awash with adverts for these: 'Click here if you're over 40 and have a bad back', coupled with an image of an attractive woman swinging a golf club. Now that may be great marketing, but this kind of swing is entirely unnecessary.

The simple fact is that if you have a bad back purely from playing golf, then you're swinging the club incorrectly. As legendary teacher Bob Toski advises, 'If you shift your weight to your left on the downswing, and let your right heel come off the ground, you should be able to play forever.'

So don't adopt a new 'back-friendly' and ugly swing – which will also lose you fifty yards of distance. Do a few simple stretches to keep your shoulder turn strong, making sure you get through the ball into a classic 'belt-buckle-pointing-at-the-target' follow-through, and you should have no issues.

30. Stay fluid

Another great lesson to learn from observing pros and amateurs is the conscious fluidity that a pro keeps as they address the ball, versus the unconscious tension that an amateur creates.

There are a lot of ways to gain this fluidity and sense of relaxation in your swing. One is to do a Jason Dufner and waggle first. I'm quite a fan of this – and, let's not forget, he adopted it after watching Hogan and Snead as he grew up. You're in good company with that trio.

Jack Nicklaus always kept his club an inch or so above the grass and maintains it works for a couple of reasons: it stops him catching the club on the way back, and it forces him to take it back smoothly.

The process I use, partly described in the pre-shot routine section (Tip 10), involves me staying fluid whilst approaching the ball. Waggling very briefly, just to ease any tension, I then do a small forward press. I've done this ever since I was a small boy and the analogy that was given to me then, which sticks with me to this day, is to think of a water bucket in my hands. If you want to pull a bucket of water back and not spill any of it, you need to sweep it slightly the wrong way first. That sensation of a really smooth pendulum motion is exactly what I want. I want my take-away to be almost like Sam Snead's or Bobby Jones's – and you can see all three of us on the website.

31. Everything revolves around the pitch

In my rarely humble opinion, mastering the simple pitch shot is the key to mastering all the physical aspects of golf. The pitch sits as a perfect halfway house between a putt and a full swing with the driver. It has all the details of both and yet little of the complexity and frustration that the extremes can create. If you can absolutely nail a short – perhaps thirty- or forty-yard – pitch, you can very easily dial this down into a simple chip by keeping your arms and wrists more rigid. A stiff-armed chip is little more than a long putt.

Likewise, it's extremely easy to extend a short pitch into a longer pitch with a three-quarter backswing and a slightly longer follow-through. You'll gradually find that your weight moves more evenly between both feet with these shots in exactly the same way that it does with a putt.

So, how do you put this theory into practice? Well, simply take some measurements of putting performance and driving performance – and then get to work! Once you have these measurements in place, accept that you're going to go very deep into perfecting your pitching action.

I had a long conversation with Jim McLellan about how to do these pitches. He said, 'If you put a novice golfer in a field with a club and a ball and give him enough reason to learn, he or she will figure it out themselves pretty quickly.' This may sound flippant but it's a point of view that is very hard to argue with. Most of us were never taught how to throw a ball properly. When we were young we just kind of figured it out!

There are two key stages in the work to improve your pitching:

Stage One

Go to the range and mentally mark an object approximately forty yards away from you. Now take dead aim and focus very hard on reducing the distance from this point that your balls land. You'll need to feel comfortable going into Zen monk mode here. Summon up some of the golfing gods from the past and have them stand beside you, quietly urging you on. As ever, Ben Hogan is the imaginary friend with the most to offer! Once you feel you're making progress and are regularly firing balls into a reasonably small area, then it's time to move on to

Stage Two

Go to a piece of waste ground or some part of the practice area where the surface isn't so good. Hit the balls in the same way, but focus on making a great contact. It will be much harder practising here than in the rarefied atmosphere of the range, but it will remove any flaws you may have developed in the ball contact whilst using the mats. Range mats very often fool to such an extent that people excessively practising on them strike the ball very 'fat' once out on the course.

Now simply go back and take your measurements again with the full swing and with your putter. Inevitably these will be better than they were before.

Any time I feel my swing or ball contact is a little off, I head to the local par three course very early in the morning, before it's open, and find some rough ground to hit pitch shots from. I focus more on the fifty-yard mark these days because at that distance it's easier to see problems with ball flight. But, of course, you can do what you want and feel comfortable with.

> If I had a bunch of juniors, I'd teach them to play from the green backward. Short shots first, with emphasis on how to meet the ball solidly. I'd make them touch the green, then walk backwards to the tee to touch the tee, and explain why holes are designed the way they are. Then I'd teach them why everything works – why a putter has so little loft, why the sand wedge is thicker on the bottom than the pitching wedge, and why woods are larger than irons. Those things mean something.
>
> **MOE NORMAN**

If your putting starts to go south, practise hitting short chips from just off the green. When you chip, you pay a lot of attention to making the ball roll perfectly end over end. Practising that will make your putting stroke come back overnight.

BILLY CASPER

32. Putting – be very, very still

At his peak, nobody could get close to Tiger when it came to putts that really mattered. You could bet the bank that if there was an eight-foot putt which he absolutely had to make to close out a major, he'd drill it home. It was remarkable to watch, and I clearly remember wondering if we'd ever see that sort of putting ability again. Now I wonder if we'll ever even see it again from Tiger. But that's another story!

We've touched on Tiger's putting drills elsewhere, but one simple tip you can take, and immediately apply to your game, is to model how he stands over the ball for these putts. I used to copy the Seve Ballesteros stance when putting. After all it worked pretty well for him, so it seemed like a decent option. But having watched Tiger confidently hole a number of huge putts one weekend, I decided to adopt a stance and action much more similar to his. So, during my next round of golf, I stood a little more upright and kept myself almost unnaturally still during the stroke. I kept my hands as soft as ever on the grip, an aspect of their putting that Tiger and Seve had in common. The results were remarkable: a huge increase in confidence and considerably fewer putts per round than my previous attempts.

So, if you're looking to make some very quick improvements to your score, this is an almost guaranteed way to do it. And it requires no practice at all. Just a little bit of time watching Tiger on YouTube!

And if you want to prove it to yourself, to help boost your own putting confidence, then get out on to the practice green and hit ten or twenty balls with your normal stroke from about six feet. Measure the number that go in. Now putt the same number of balls, channelling Tiger and staying incredibly still.

I hold my breath during and just prior to making the [putting] stroke. Preventing the diaphragm from moving helps me to keep my body and head perfectly still.

JACK NICKLAUS, *Golf Digest*, 1972

33. Avoid the Big Miss

Numerous fascinating stories emerged from Hank Haney's excellent 2013 book about his years with Tiger, *The Big Miss*. Amongst all the interesting stories was one simple and excellent piece of information: at the very top level in golf, what most of the best players are doing is patiently working their way around the courses and attempting to avoid the 'big miss' – legendary scoring machine Ray Floyd calls it 'the big mistake'.

Haney's frustration was that Tiger couldn't accept that he should aim for a slightly less powerful and long ball off the tee, and focus instead on keeping the ball on the fairway. He was constantly trying to create a tee shot that would keep him ahead of the young guys who were starting to out-drive him. But, as we all know, when Tiger plays cautiously and keeps the ball on the fairway, he's effectively unbeatable. His imperious control of the 2006 Open at Royal Liverpool is the perfect example of that. In 72 holes he used his driver once. It was this style of cautious play that Haney promoted.

Halfway through my challenge I learnt a tremendous amount from one round of golf with a friend, Mark MacMurray, who has a handicap of plus one. My driving was very good at this stage and I was consistently longer off the tee than Mark. He'd had a lay-off for about six months due to medical issues, so was a little rusty. But by the third hole, he was level par and I was two or three strokes over. His rusty game was saved on those three first holes by exceptional skills round the green.

On the short fourth hole, a downhill driveable par four, I pulled out the driver and blasted it down the fairway in an effort to show him how great I was. I landed in the bunker. He pulled out his three wood and dropped it about sixty yards short of the green. I made par and he birdied.

For the rest of the round he cautiously picked his way round the course and returned a par round; I shot in the mid-eighties. But the lesson stuck with me: at heart I remain an aggressive golfer, but I play in a much more cautious way. Mark knew his game was off and worked around it. He expertly avoided any trouble, and the occasional little problems were saved by his incredible short game. There are many ways to shoot par, and many of them require intelligence and thoughtfulness as much as your 'A game' in play. Prove this to yourself by going out armed with nothing more than your 'easiest to hit' hybrid club and no long irons. For the average amateur golfer, even to the single-figure handicap level, this will almost certainly produce a better round than they had previously been averaging.

Think about your last few rounds and count how many shots you lost by losing balls or shooting into trees, water or fields. If you could prevent all of those, but perhaps be fifty yards shorter off the tee and lay up to a few more greens, you would have scored better. As ever, it's worth a test. One round of golf in which your only mission is to avoid trouble and the 'big miss' – and then see how you can incorporate what you've learned into your game in the future.

34. Understand the power of great course management

A handful of books have transformed the way I play golf, and one, in particular, had an enormous impact: Raymond Floyd's *The Elements of Scoring*. Written in 1998, it now languishes deep down the golf bestseller charts on Amazon and can be hard to find in traditional bookshops.

There's a statement at the start of the book that particularly sticks with me. Ray writes: 'If somehow I was given your physical (golf) game, and we had a match, I would beat you 99 times out of 100. Because I know how to play the game better than you do.'

It may sound arrogant – probably permissible if you've won four majors – but it's also extremely profound. If you can think of that phrase and imagine you're Ray on the back nine of a major before every shot, I think we both know you'll shoot a better round than normal.

The critical lesson is to realise that you have two choices at the start of every round. Choice one is where you play your usual game and adopt your normal attitude towards risk and reward. Choice two, the Ray Floyd approach, is to completely accept your limitations and play each hole with great thought on how to score well.

I heartily recommend Ray's book but, in essence, that's what it boils down to – playing with your head rather than your heart.

35. Know, to the yard, exactly how far you hit the ball with each of your clubs

In the months leading up to my challenge, I started reading a few golf magazines again. It had been over twenty years since I'd bought one and they were at once very familiar and also very different to those I remembered. The number of adverts at the back was the same, but the enormous variety of clubs and aids contained within them was very different.

I recognised very few of the golfers who appeared, and most of the technical swing articles went completely over my head. Initially I felt little or no desire to get back into golf. But I persevered and, over a few months, I started to get my enthusiasm for the game back. One of the magazines featured a monthly column in which a famous touring professional gave their best advice to amateur golfers, based on their experiences of playing in pro-ams. For four months in a row, all the professionals said the biggest mistakes they saw were amateurs under-clubbing, and overestimating the distance they could hit the ball.

This is one of the most effective lessons you can learn. It's not always easy to find the physical space to record these measurements, but with a little creativity it is very possible. And if you decide you can't find somewhere to do it, then you probably don't really care enough about improving!

There was no practice area at Blackwood where I could measure these distances properly. I was forced to use a number of different places to piece together accurate results. I paced out distances on both the main Hamilton course and also on the par three course. I also got up very early, went to my local pitch and putt (before it opened) and measured them for several mornings. I spent time in a field beside a course once, too, using the best piece of grass I could find to hit from.

The advantage of taking the measurements in different places is that you end up with a proper set of averages. Different balls, different wind, different levels of run and grass condition will all produce a different result. But eventually your little notebook will have a genuine and trustworthy average for each club. And it's unlikely to be the same number that you had in your head. That number is likely to be based on perfect conditions and a perfect strike.

Once you have completed this work, when you stand 150 yards from the pin you can, with proper quantifiable evidence, know whether you need a six, seven or eight iron based on your research. And that knowledge will stand you in great stead.

Ultimately, though, this information is worthless unless you have a really solid grasp of exactly how far you are from the pin. When visiting a new course, I make a point of asking in the pro shop what the distance markers relate to. They are sometimes based on the distance to the front edge and equally often to a point in the middle of the green. I know from experience that, even if I'm playing with a member of that course, they rarely know which of the two it is. I spent a solid couple of months making sure that my pace was an accurate yard in an effort to make sure I was capable of getting my distance to the markers correct so, at a new course, I measure from the first hole markers to the green to make sure that the information I was given is correct. I'm aware that is a little OCD too!

Having this information, along with your best guess as to where the pin is in relation to the distance measurement, allows you to stand over the ball with more confidence than the average club golfer. And we all know just how powerful confidence can be in terms of your ball striking.

In the pro-ams I play in, I've hardly ever seen an amateur hit a shot long. It's not unusual when I'm playing in scrambles to watch amateurs hit less club than me from the same spot, even though their best drives have been finishing 75 yards short of mine. When I ask them to tell me the last time they were over the green with their approach, they can't remember.

RAY FLOYD

36. Play some rounds of golf with different objectives

Karl Morris – mind coach to Darren Clarke, Lee Westwood and Graeme McDowell – taught me the value of playing games with different objectives in mind. Karl talks about having a little tick box, either real or imagined, beside each hole on your score card. In this box you have to put a little tick if you've completed the objective for that hole. Your priority for the round is not the score; it's about having 18 little ticks. If you have 18 little ticks, you can regard the round as being a success.

I first used Karl's system to ensure I applied my full pre-shot routine before every single shot. I'm a very easily distracted golfer (and human being in general) so this was a great way to force me to maintain my routine, even on the later holes on the back nine when my focus tends to waver. The first time I did it, I saw a marked improvement on my scores.

But there are lots of other ways to look at objectives for a round, all of which should help you focus on improving your game, rather than beating your partners on any specific day. You might decide that you are going to play an extremely cautious round, for example, with a tick applied if every shot on each hole was carefully considered and executed, allowing you to anticipate and avoid potential trouble.

Or you might decide to use your round to make notes on the perfect way to play each hole: plotting your way around the course as if it were a blank sheet of paper – like a great caddie walking it for the first time. Perhaps you'll decide to focus purely on keeping a 6 off your card, or on two-putting, or on systematically addressing all the variables – such as wind, grass condition and possible issues with the various landing surfaces – before each shot.

All of this will help you place each round within the larger context of an overall improvement process, and remove the worries about individual scores. And as you start to make more ticks, you'll know that you're moving towards a much better game. As the story below illustrates, you can sometimes be amazed at just how well you score when you remove the pressure to score. It's counterintuitive, but a useful bonus.

 JOHN'S TRUE STORIES

The first par round of golf I ever played was actually a bit of an accident. It was on a par-three course – I was there to check and refine the distances I'd been hitting my irons – and I had no witnesses, so it didn't count towards my Dream On challenge, but there are a couple of great lessons contained within the story.

It happened on the Temple course at Blackwood. It's a proper par three course, not a glorified pitch and putt, so it has some properly challenging and decently long holes. I could play 18 holes of golf in about two hours there – the time I would take to play 9 holes on the full course – meaning

I could also spend some time on the range with my driver. In about three hours I would make substantial progress with my golf.

So with that in mind, most of my par three rounds were test sessions where I would experiment with new ideas. Perhaps I'd choose to play all my fifty yards and in shots with a lob wedge, then the next day I'd reverse that decision and play those same shots with a straight-armed chipping stroke and a nine iron. These rounds were played with a notebook in my back pocket, and a desire to place another piece into the complicated jigsaw of effective scoring by the end. I didn't always manage to slot that piece home, but I certainly succeeded more often than I failed.

On this particular occasion I was attempting to gain complete control of my iron distances. That meant that in certain situations I deliberately used the wrong club off the tee. I might play an eight iron simply because I wanted to get the distance nailed in my book, rather than the correct seven iron for the hole, because I was confident of that distance. This meant that often I wasn't quite reaching the green or sometimes I was going a bit long. But that didn't worry me at all, because the outcome wasn't the score, it was simply to nail the distances. But, of course, I did keep score …

On the sixteenth tee, I realised, with a jolt, that I was standing at level par, but I couldn't quite grasp how this could be, as I didn't think I'd been playing particularly spectacular golf. On the previous hole I'd deliberately played short and only just scrambled a par. So I checked through the card to see if there had been any mistakes in keeping score – but there weren't. I really was sitting at level par.

So I decided to really focus on parring the last three holes and, incredibly, I managed it! It was a fascinating example of how, by focusing on different outcomes, you can end up with a brilliant score.

. . . .

37. Slow it down

I know, I know, whatever next – 'Drive for show, putt for dough'? But the annoying fact about clichés like this one is that in so many cases, they're based on solid evidence and results.

Almost every time I have an issue with my swing while out on the course, I can mostly fix it by dropping my swing speed down to about 80 per cent. I may not fully know what I've fixed, but as long as I can get round the course without getting into too much trouble I'm happy to have taken a few yards off my tee shots and from each iron.

I experimented a lot at the range to see how much I could slow my driver swing down without losing distance. The answer is a surprisingly large amount. Try it yourself and see. Go to the range and attempt ten shots between two markers that are roughly the size of a fairway. Hit the ball at a swing speed of about 95 per cent (about as hard as you can hit it but while still keeping a decent balance) and measure both the approximate average distance of each shot, and how many balls you can strike between the two markers.

Now do the same thing at about 75–80 per cent and take the same measurements. I can bet money on the fact that you'll not have lost much more than about ten yards, and will definitely have a higher count between the two markers.

What you've now done is proven to yourself that

you really don't lose that much distance with an easier and more controlled swing. And this should absolutely become your default swing with all irons. If you ever feel you are even slightly close to falling back after an iron shot, then you haven't taken enough club. I watched the exceptional coach and commentator Simon Holmes go into a bewildered rant on television after he'd watched Alviro Quiros and Anthony Kim, two incredibly talented young golfers, lashing their nine irons well over 150 yards, both landing well away from the flag. He was incredulous as to why they would do that, when an eight iron could have been hit in a much more controlled manner. It just shows that, even at this level, golfers can make mistakes that waste their talent.

Ray Floyd talks about how most professional golfers only hit at about 85 per cent, and if you watch any decent pro over the age of thirty-five, you'll see he is correct. The young guns may still lash out a bit and get caught up in alpha male distance competitions, but the older guys know that ball control and a balanced swing will always be more important.

So, if those guys are not hitting more than 85 per cent, why are you?

A little drill to help you with this

Go to the range with a friend who will agree to help you strike the ball at differing levels of effort. That doesn't necessarily mean speed or size of backswing/ follow-through, it simply means the amount of effort that is felt by you in swinging the club.

Ask your friend to randomly shout out percentage figures (70, 30, 80 per cent etc), and then try to strike the ball with that amount of effort. After each shot make sure you take a step back and 'shake it out' so you're fresh for the next strike and not too affected by the previous one. Methodically work your way through about fifty balls using this process, keeping yourself fresh with frequent sips of water and a little stretching as you go along.

Once you're finished, and being as honest with yourself as you can, work out which percentage produced the best quality of ball strike to distance ratio. You'd be surprised at how often that can be as low as 50 per cent. It's never over 80 per cent though, and we've proved this out in various 'Dream On' clinics around the country.

38. Grip down an inch and know how much this affects your distance

Experiment with the grip on your driver and see how much accuracy you gain – and how much distance you lose. As ever, it's very useful to prove this on the range, but it's a tip that can be used on the course if the wheels are falling off on a round.

I lose about ten yards off the tee by gripping down an inch on my driver, but it vastly increases my confidence, and also makes me much more likely to keep it on the fairway. In fact I have found this method so effective that, instead of holding it in reserve for when I am in trouble, it is now the only way I drive the ball. I could, of course, get a shorter driver (and don't forget Tiger now uses a driver an inch and a half shorter than he did earlier in his career) but there's a psychological advantage, in my mind at least, to looking down and seeing that I'm gripping down the club. It makes me feel that the ball is easier to hit.

I've also experimented with all my short irons and wedges, and I know that gripping an inch down will generally give me a shot that is ten yards shorter than I would normally hit with that club. So an eight iron gripped down an inch will get me about 140 yards, and that fills a gap between the 150 yards I hit my normal eight iron, and the 135 yards I hit my nine iron.

Likewise, an inch down on my pitching wedge will get me 115 yards, whereas my gap wedge will only normally shoot about 105–110 yards. All of this dramatically improves my confidence in the club in my hand and helps me to produce the same controlled swing and reach the distance I need. From 150 yards and in, and when coupled with the clock face routine, I can be very sure that I will get it close to the flag.

39. Get the clubs that help you score

There is almost no end to the discussions on this subject. You can easily get lost in shaft technology and seduced by the endless tweaks that a good club fitter can provide. But I, at the risk of offending some exceptional club fitters and manufacturers, am going to keep it very simple. If you choose to do otherwise, well, that's your prerogative: but expect to spend a lot of money.

I set out with a number of key rules in my challenge and, by and large, I stuck to them. One of those rules was that I wouldn't contemplate buying new clubs, or get enticed by new technology, until I had created a new swing and could look myself in the mirror and say 'okay, you're now a decent golfer'. That arbitrary and, frankly, easy to fudge, measure, was also backed up by a quantifiable one – I needed to have broken 80.

To ensure that I didn't break this rule I made sure that I didn't align myself with any club manufacturers and get myself fitted for what they felt was the latest and greatest set of clubs. That may seem counter-productive, but the image in my mind was of great golfers like Ben Hogan, Jack Nicklaus and Seve Ballesteros producing rounds of golf that still leave us in awe, using equipment that most modern professionals would struggle to break par with. Was that the correct way to look at it? Well, ever since I completed my challenge, there have been a number of high-profile attempts by others to match what I did.

Most of these people have chosen to use sponsored clubs (a remarkably easy thing to organise) – and not one of them has come close to breaking par.

When that glorious sub-80 round was produced, I decided that it was finally time to spend a little money and park the twenty-year-old Mizuno irons borrowed from my late father-in-law, and the fifteen-year-old Big Bertha borrowed from my brother-in-law. I also decided that the putter I'd found in the starters hut at Blackwood probably could be replaced by something that gave me more confidence.

The details of the clubs I changed to are largely irrelevant – they are listed in *Dream On*, should you want to know – but what does matter here is that I decided to get clubs that were as easy as possible to hit, and that would inspire me with confidence. That meant standing at the range and hitting a LOT of balls with sample six irons, and choosing wedges that just felt good in my hands.

I did see a substantial improvement when I tried out the more modern drivers – the technology on drivers moves so fast that it would have been impossible not to – but I ended up with a TaylorMade model that comfortably added an astonishing thirty yards to my drives.

Over the next few months I tweaked and amended what I was doing, and made a few mistakes along the way: I foolishly lost about a month of progress by thinking the lob wedge was some sort of gift from God to the golfing masses. I blame Seve for this, because he felt they gave the modern professional such an advantage that they should be banned. Rather stupidly, I hadn't grasped that he wasn't talking about me, or any average club golfer! The lob wedge is a great piece of kit, but only once you've really mastered your short game feel, and only in certain situations, such as the need to get the ball high and land softly on a small putting surface.

In the end I managed to amass a set of clubs that not only increased my confidence on the course but suited both my game and (equally as important) the course that I was attempting the challenge on. My core bag consisted of:

- Driver – 8.5 degrees, X shaft

- Three wood – 15 degrees, stiff shaft

- Rescue/hybrid – 22 degrees

- Rescue/hybrid – 24 degrees

- Cavity back 'game improvement irons' – five to pitching wedge

- Matched wedges – 52/56/60 degrees

- Best selling putter in the world!

It's worth bearing in mind that, even with this somewhat parsimonious attitude, I had nine wedges in the house at one stage, and more than five drivers.

But, if you ignore my obvious hypocrisy, what I was really trying to do was focus on my strengths (short game) and ignore my weaknesses (long irons). I ended up with a driver that really suited me, although it wasn't the longest off the tee. And my wedges allowed me to fully exploit the clock face routine that became so important to my game.

The 22-degree hybrid was also the perfect club to help me reach the 210-yard par three third hole at Blackwood. My three wood, even when choking down, was consistently too long for this hole, so the hybrid helped me confidently stand on the tee of this tough hole and feel like I had a real chance of making par. And that's proof that confidence can sometimes be bought!

So my advice is to choose a set of clubs that really work for *you*. Ignore the fancy adverts, ignore whatever new clubs your favourite golfer has just turned to, and consider what help *your* game might need. I don't care (well I do a bit if I'm honest …) that my friends accuse me of being a girl because I have two hybrids: ultimately, I really only care about the score. And so should you. Make that your priority when choosing clubs.

40. Practise your three-foot putt ...

Many years ago, Phil Mickelson asked Jackie Burke, who is regarded as one of the greatest putters of all time, for his advice on putting. Jackie was a great golfer, but also a very blunt talker and he doesn't believe in clever tricks or secrets. Like my own mentor, Jim McLellan, he believes that if you put enough pressure on yourself, you'll eventually work out how to pitch or putt the ball.

So he told Mickelson what he told everyone else: to go out and hole 100 three-foot putts in a row. That's what Jackie himself did every night to stay sharp. He is a small guy, and knew he couldn't compete with the big boys on distance; therefore he had no option but to be a brilliant putter. He would set twelve balls at a time around the practice pin, lining them up like the numbers on a clock, and methodically work his way round, holing one after another.

Mickelson was confident, and bet Jackie 'the finest dinner in Houston' that he would be able to do it on his first attempt, but he missed the fourth putt. In fact, it took Mickelson two months to complete the drill with 100 putts in a row. But who can argue with his results, as putting has become the cornerstone of his game. His short game is all geared toward putting the ball into that three-foot zone. That way, when the pressure is on, he knows that he can stand over the ball and feel confident that he'll get it into the hole.

It's an exceptional drill to try, and a very useful way to look at your game. The pressure increases as you get closer and closer to the 100 mark, but that's the key to any practice. You *must* put yourself under pressure.

Make sure you check out the video that accompanies this section to hear Jackie talking through the story. It's a fascinating glimpse into a little piece of history.

41. ... and your six-foot putt

I told you at the beginning that there might appear to be contradictory tips and ideas within this book, so I thought I'd put two of them right beside each other. It's a useful way to illustrate that you need to take from these tips the ideas and drills that work for and resonate with you. If a certain tip doesn't seem to click with you then move on and try another one. This particular tip is just another great way of looking at your putting and short game and, in my opinion anyway, is possibly more relevant to the average golfer than the Mickelson/Burke 100 putts drill. But as with all the tips, you should try the drill for yourself and make up your own mind.

Ray Floyd regards the six-foot putt as the most important putt in golf. He maintains that if you can make putts consistently and confidently from that range then you dramatically improve your ability to score. If you're sound from six feet you've widened your target for chips, pitches and long putts to a twelve-foot diameter circle. And that's a very easy target.

Surprisingly perhaps, the average tour pro only holes about 50 per cent of putts from this distance, and the average amateur less than 33 per cent. Your goal, according to Floyd, is to attempt to get as close as possible to the 50 per cent mark.

I stand somewhere between the two camps on this. My ability to (mostly) get all shots from fifty yards and in within a three-foot radius of the hole is, without a shadow of a doubt, the best skill I have developed in golf. I know that from around that range, certainly twenty yards or so, I'll get it within the three-foot zone – and therefore feel capable of getting up and down and perhaps rescuing a few erratic shots from earlier in the hole.

But in terms of putting practice, I think there's a lot to be said for practising those six-foot putts. Dealing with statistics and gradually trying to improve them, rather than expecting perfection like in the 100-ball Burke drill, works better for me.

But, again, you must work out what is better for *you*. Not just at a gut level, but also what translates into actual quantifiable results – both on the practice green and on the course. It doesn't really matter what you choose though. Putting work into your three-foot, six-foot, or even four-and-a-half foot putts, on a consistent basis, cannot fail to improve your golf.

42. Correctly manage the par five

Par-five holes tend to panic the average high handicapper. Golfers focus on the length of the hole, rather than the number of shots allocated to play it, and throw all reason to the wind. They stare off into the distance muttering words like 'monster' and 'nightmare' and, in what can only be an attempt to try and 'tame the monster', they make the mistake of blasting their driver as hard as they can. You don't need me to tell you what the average results of that are.

A few years ago I read an article which suggested that an 18 handicapper would score, on average, better on par fives by hitting three seven irons rather than going down the traditional route of driver, three wood and wedge. I found this fascinating and tried it out on the course several times in the early part of my challenge, and I suggest you do the same just to test it out.

It's a very peculiar feeling standing on the tee, staring off at a green in the distance, with only a weedy little seven iron in your hands. Especially if you know your partner will probably blast a shot 280 yards down the fairway with his driver. But the first time I tried this tip was actually quite satisfying – after mocking me quite relentlessly for my choice in club, my partner managed to blast his drive in a lovely arcing hook ... straight into the water. Suddenly my beautifully placed seven-iron shot about 160 yards up the fairway didn't look so foolish. A second seven iron took me past the 300-yard mark, and the third put me onto the green. Two putts, and a par was in the bag.

Bear in mind that at this stage I was still a classic bogey golfer and I would normally have played that hole like this: drive off the tee and hopefully into safety; three wood off the fairway, either into rough or about forty yards short of green. If I'd managed to get the bunker I'd almost certainly struggle, as most golfers do, with the long bunker shot, and fluff it short of the green. That would leave me having to up and down for par.

So you'll see that, even though I was driving the ball a long way in those days, I was still struggling to make par on a relatively short and easy par five. All three times I attempted the seven iron experiment I got a nice round par with no lost ball and no sense of a big miss.

This experiment is an extreme way of illustrating that you really shouldn't be intimidated by a par five, and that the course should be seen as a blank sheet. On each hole try to avoid all preconceived notions of what should or shouldn't be played. The logical step up from the seven iron is to hit the longest club you have in your bag that you feel (with about 90 per cent accuracy) you can avoid all trouble with. For me that's my 22-degree hybrid as I have created something of a 'go to' shot (see next tip) with this club. I know that with it and with a certain type of swing, I'll be able to hit just over 200 yards all day long. And maybe only 5 per cent of those will veer into trouble: pretty good odds in my opinion.

But let's add a little context to it: Tiger Woods' accuracy off the tee varies between about mid-fifties to low sixties in percentage terms. That means that, on average, Tiger is missing four fairways in every ten, or two out of every five. Very often when Tiger stands on the tee, his odds of hitting the fairway are only about 50 per cent. At the time of writing, Zach Johnson is the most accurate player on tour, and yet even he is only hitting 76 per cent of fairways which translates as three out of four balls on the fairway.

So, even though I am probably exaggerating my 95 per cent accuracy, I am at least as accurate off the tee as Zach Johnson. I'll be about 75 yards shorter than him, obviously, but let's also note that I don't play 7,200-yard courses very often. In fact, the courses I play are probably about 1,000 yards shorter than that on average – so approximately 55 yards shorter on each hole.

What I mean is that I can be more accurate than a player like Zach Johnson and perhaps be only about 20 yards behind him on the fairway in scoring terms. I'm acutely aware that there are multiple flaws with this argument. But, for the purpose of this test, ignore them and think about how *you* can craft a game with your clubs, whether you're on a par five or not, that will give you a sizeable advantage over your playing partners, who stick with their conventional 'club and hole' choice.

So, if I then take another shot with my 22-degree hybrid, I'm now about 400 yards down the fairway on the par five – and assuming my 95 per cent accuracy with this club is correct, I have a 90 per cent chance (95% x 95%) that I'll be in a good position. And even if I'm being overly generous in my figures and I can only hit 90 per cent of those safety hybrid shots, that still leaves me with an 81 per cent chance (90% x 90%) of being right on the fairway with about 100 yards to go! Those are odds I quite like, especially since that is right in my three-quarter pitching wedge zone – another shot I'm extremely happy with.

Now, I'm no Zach Johnson, I never will be, and I'll never win the Masters, but this was the sort of thinking that helped me take 33 strokes off my game in one year. And it's also the sort of thinking that *you* can apply to your own game.

A particularly successful colleague once gave me this bit of business advice: 'It's *your* box of tricks – you should always remember that and realise that the business is there to craft in whatever way you want, not in the way that others believe you should.' The golf course and your clubs are your 'bag of tricks' – never feel you should play them in the 'accepted' way.

 # JOHN'S TRUE STORIES

The Zach Johnson Masters Strategy

Zach Johnson, in the year that he won the Masters (2007) was a prime example of a player challenging accepted wisdom.

Over the previous decade Augusta had ballooned in length and was considered almost unwinnable unless you had the sort of distance that Tiger and the up-and-coming players had. The only winning strategy seemed to be to try and beat the course into submission, reach all the par fives in two shots and hopefully rack up a few birdies along the way.

The problem is, as you almost certainly know, Augusta doesn't lend itself well to shots that aren't pinpoint accurate. Just having the distance to reach the greens in two is a long way away from safely getting a birdie or even par. There is a tremendous amount of trouble around those greens and even positioning yourself on the wrong level of the green can lead to danger.

So Zach Johnson planned out a different strategy and decided to not attempt any of the par fives in two. He was going to lay up for each of them and use his exceptional short game to hopefully get into a position where he could hole a few putts and score a few birdies. He managed it beautifully, and on Sunday afternoon there he was having Phil Mickelson help him on with the green jacket.

. . . .

43. Develop a 'go to' shot

This, in my opinion, is one of the easiest ways for a high handicapper to drop three or four strokes in a couple of weeks. It's a classic 20 per cent tip. You absolutely will get a tangible result if you put this in your armoury.

Many years ago, a pro golfer friend of mine went to Dallas for a year or two to improve his game. He had enormous natural talent, but needed to refine not just his shot making, but also his mental attitude. Whilst there, he hung out with a number of the guys on the tour, and practised regularly with them, both on the course and on the range.

He told me a story about Bruce Lietzke, who despite having multiple wins was not one of those golfers that practised relentlessly and whose whole life was devoted to golf. He was a strongly committed family man and had created a game plan to allow him to keep both his free time and his card.

One morning Lietzke was practising on the range with my friend nearby. Again and again he hit the same wedge shot to about 90 yards. My friend practised for a while and then went about some other business and had his lunch. Many hours later he strolled back down to the range to see Lietzke still hitting the exact same shot. It had been six full hours – on one shot!

My friend was both intrigued by this, and in awe of Lietzke's dedication. When questioned about it, Lietzke said that he wanted to create a shot in which he had total confidence. He practised very little else in his game apart from that one shot and his short game. It meant that on a par five he could always play safe and leave it 90 yards from the pin on his second shot. His ability to get up and down from that range was incredible, as that 90-yard shot was so heavily ingrained within his game. It also meant that on a tricky and long par four (perhaps with water in front of the green) he could do the same thing and, most of the time, still save par.

When my friend first told me this, I was fascinated. It was many years before my *Dream On* challenge, but it was a principle that I incorporated into my business life. And when I did start my challenge, I knew I had to get my own 'go to' shot. For me it became a 3/4 sand wedge which I could play to 67 yards with military precision. It's still a shot I have enormous confidence in. I've since adjusted it a little so it's now my pitching wedge with the same swing to give me about 95 yards and it allows me a little more flexibility on the longer courses.

I hadn't seen my friend for a few years, and when we spoke recently we chatted about his experience in Dallas. His 'go to' shot is very similar to Lietzke's. It's a punched 52-degree wedge that bounces twice and stops. And yet he acknowledges that he often doesn't rely on it, preferring instead (like so many of us) to attack aggressively most of the time. He knows that he'll up and down from that distance more often than not.

The principle is great for many reasons. Not least of which is the fact that when your swing is bad or you're having a bad day, you will nearly always be able to go to this shot and hit it with some confidence. That's why it makes most sense to develop it with a club that's relatively easy to hit, like a very short iron or wedge. When all seems lost you can use this shot to bolster your confidence, and gradually that confidence will seep back into the rest of your game.

With this in mind I created another 'go to' shot of 200 yards with my 22-degree hybrid – the exact shot that I describe in Tip 42, the par five tip. I don't have quite the same confidence in it as I have in my wedges, but I've measured extensively and can hit this shot onto the fairway with 95 per cent accuracy. It's not quite a full shot, so the swing is a nice gentle motion that allows me to stay relaxed.

On top of this, to perhaps slightly overly extend the single 'go to' shot concept, I developed another version with my eight iron. With this, the two wedges, and my hybrid, I now have four shots in my bag that I feel very comfortable with – not winning-a-PGA-tour-title confident, but confident enough for me!

Almost no matter how weak our game is, we can (if we work at it) hit a good 3/4 wedge. A 24 handicapper could reliably hit a 3/4 wedge very, very quickly if that was all he focused on for three or four range sessions – building a level of confidence which will help him to bumble his way round most par fours and fives with rescue clubs or short irons, and still save par (hopefully) by bashing a wedge to six feet. Depending on your current standards, this one tip alone could help you scramble round your own course in a more effective fashion and could even knock three or four strokes off your average round. Don't underestimate it just because it doesn't seem a glamorous technique.

When Jack Nicklaus is hitting the ball poorly he says he is prepared to stand on the tee and go right down the bag as far as the wedge until he feels comfortable hitting the ball. I doubt he has ever had to actually do that, but the belief that he can always hit his wedge well no matter how badly he is striking the ball, and the lack of concern for what others think, helps to stop him hitting driver or long irons when his game is a little off.

That's why I originally chose the eight iron: because I have such confidence in that club, I know that I will always be able to hit some good shots, no matter how bad a day I'm having. This allows me to take things a lot easier off the tee and let myself scramble a bit. It also lets me take my rescue club off the tee if I'm shooting badly and not keep working away at the driver.

A rescue club at 200 yards, and two 150-yard eight irons, still allows me to be on a par five green in three shots. A rescue and an eight allows me to get pretty close on lots of par fours too, and if my short game is still okay I can still hope for an up and down.

But there's another advantage too. Having a 'go to' shot stops you attempting some of those crazy shots out of trees after a wayward drive and gives you the confidence to know that a safe chip out to about the 150 yard on the fairway will still give you a decent chance of par.

44. Practise with a 50 pence coin

During the winter months, and on those evenings when I couldn't get out to the range, I developed a bad habit of chipping balls from the carpet onto the sofa. The balls that missed caused a horrendous clatter when they landed on our wooden floors and, after a stern chat from both my wife and daughter, I decided to employ a tip suggested by the late Peter Dobereiner – I started to use a 50 pence piece instead of a ball. It was much quieter, and did the job nicely!

With the coin being so small, you need a very controlled swing in order to make clean contact and hoist it onto your sofa (or whatever your indoor target happens to be). When you finally get out and onto the course again, the ball will seem a ludicrously easy thing to hit by comparison. It's incredible how both your confidence and striking ability can take a serious leap forward with this quirky but simple tip. And here's another tip! If you also have wooden floors, find yourself an old scrap of carpet to strike your coin from – this will help you avoid that difficult 'chat' with your spouse!

This technique works well within my 'make practice harder than play' philosophy too, and it allowed me to get a little practice in while I watched that week's supply of eBay video purchases.

45. Practise slowly, with a weighted club

One of the most crucial things you must be able to do is to groove through any swing changes. As I've discussed previously, this must always be done away from the course – but I'm aware it isn't always possible to get to the range, or work through the drills in peace.

When I couldn't get to the range, to help groove in any improvements I would use my weighted club – which was generally an old five iron with a weight taped onto the club face. There are multiple, sometimes very expensive, weighted clubs available out there to buy, but, as you'll see from the video, any old club and a small tin of beans is all you need!

What I do is very, very slowly take a full swing with this club, making absolutely sure I am focusing on all the various positions I need to be in for the particular issue I'm working on. The swing needs to be excruciatingly slow – ideally take a full minute for each one you practise.

Using this technique something magical seemed to happen with whatever problem I was trying to deal with. When I next made it to the range or the course, the new action seemed to be almost instinctively ingrained into my swing.

It's a very useful technique if you are very short of time and just have ten minutes or so to swing a club in the garden. And it may be simple, but don't underestimate it.

One thing to be aware of: if, like me, you're getting a little creaky, make sure you warm up with an ordinary club before you start swinging with weighted clubs. It's very easy to pull muscles with weighted clubs – and you really don't want to do this as it will severely hold back the rest of your practice for a while.

46. Cure your shanks

The 'shank' is almost an unmentionable word in golf. It's the only affliction that golfers are consistently unhappy to discuss out loud.

As a child starting out in the game, it never created an issue for me. Kids may occasionally shank a ball but, being much wiser in golfing terms than adults (and I'm actually being serious when I say that), they don't suddenly think 'bugger it – I've caught the shanks and will be plagued for the foreseeable future'. They simply reload and try again.

When I got back into golf at the start of my challenge, I played a round with a cousin who told me that his brother had given up the game completely, despite reaching an 11 handicap, as a result of a bout of shanks. To me that seemed like incredibly irrational behaviour – until, of course, I encountered my first bout of the dreaded shanks myself ...

I document the bizarre situation in detail in *Dream On* but I'll briefly retell the story here. I was badly shanking at the range. A friend, who played off a six handicap, saw me and started laughing at my plight. He went into his bay and, not surprisingly, if you believe shanks folklore, he started shanking too! I obviously felt much better.

Then along came Debbie, the pro who helped me out during my challenge. She teased us a bit, then hit a few shots and, unbelievably, started shanking herself!

It was an utterly surreal situation, but I immediately

realised that a case of shanks is as much a mental issue as a physical one. And as such, it's important to deal with it as quickly as possible to stop it from becoming an issue that festers in your mind when out on the course.

The basic problem is that you are hitting the ball off the heel of the club and it catches with the hosel. Somewhere in your confused golf mind, a signal goes out which screams, 'Don't hit it off the heel, don't hit it off the heel!' But, as the psychologists tell us, the brain can't understand a negative command so what we actually hear is: 'Hit it off the heel, hit it off the heel' and so, we do …

There are a variety of solutions to this problem, but the most important thing to do is to get to the range with a full bucket of balls and exorcise the shanking demons as quickly as possible. In many ways the speed of the reaction is far more important than the actual solution.

With that said though, one of the best solutions to shanking I have come across is a David Leadbetter tip. He advises addressing the ball *starting* with the ball at the heel! This may seem counterintuitive but, as is so often the case with golf improvement tips and fixes, something counterintuitive may be the best solution.

If you address at the heel and then actively attempt to hit off the toe of the club, you are forcing yourself to use the correct swing path. This solution forces a better long-term technique than many of those which force you to avoid hitting a club cover or a tee placed beside the ball. So you're much more likely to get a result which will work and thus prevent you from hitting the course with doubt in your mind.

So remember, the key thing here is the removal of doubt. That may take ten balls, or it may take three buckets of balls, but you *must* reach the end of your session confident that you have fixed the issue.

47. Putt and miss on the 'pro side'

This tip comes from Tom Watson: one of the greatest short game experts the world has ever seen. And that, right there, is another tip. If you're serious about improving, then listen to the very best. Listen to the tips that come from the greatest golfers who've ever existed, particularly the ones who specialise or excel in whichever area it is you're trying to improve. For example, take lessons in ball striking from Sergio Garcia – but don't look to him if you want tips on how to keep a cool head on the course …!

The lesson from Tom was to putt and miss on the 'pro side'.

Tom talks about how in the weekly pro-ams he would always witness amateurs miss on the low side of a breaking putt. Almost without exception amateur golfers don't factor in enough break. But the key thing here is that if you miss on the high side, and perhaps factor in a little too much break, then the ball still has a chance to fall in – a chance that the ball on the low side simply won't have.

As I often say, it's very useful to have a specific goal to focus on when you're playing a round of golf. So the next time you're out for 18 holes, why not set yourself a challenge to factor in enough break so that you won't miss on the low side.

And then see how it affects your scores.

48. Putt to something other than the hole

This is one of those old tips that I remember from the game as a child. There are a couple of ways to do it, both of which help different parts of your putting.

The first idea is to putt to a tee. This conforms very well with the principles of hard practice that I discuss at the beginning. A tee is much smaller than a hole, so by giving yourself a more difficult target, especially for short putts, you will naturally put more pressure on yourself, and wrap that all-important myelin round those neural pathways. Practising a clock face of twelve putts to a tee three feet away will be very tough, and it will really test you. And you won't need to hit 100 in a row to a normal hole like Phil Mickelson to feel the pressure.

I challenge you to spend twenty minutes on the putting green before you go out, putting to a tee from a variety of distances – short, medium and long. Make sure you put some pressure on yourself to actually hit the tee though – there's no point in just making a game out of it. And, when you step out onto the course, the hole will look almost comically large.

The second idea is to putt to the fringe of the green to help focus on your distance control. Good putting can seem multi-faceted, but essentially it's just an equation between accuracy and distance control – two basic factors which may be interlinked, but are in many ways separate too.

49. Engage in some play practice

In Tip 9 I outline, in great detail, the importance of 'hard practice'. It was this type of practice that allowed me to make the biggest steps forward in my improvement. In 80/20 terms it's the 4 per cent that is left when you take 20 per cent of the 20 per cent. It really is an incredibly effective way to spend your time.

During this process of learning, which included reading twenty or so books on the science of how we learn and how the brain works, I did a fair amount of research into how the bonobo monkey learns. I discovered that they learn significantly faster in a play environment. And since we're remarkably close to them genetically, there clearly must be parallels in how we learn ourselves.

It's common sense really. I look back at school and know that my learning capacity was improved tenfold by inspirational teachers who taught in an engaging and entertaining way. I almost became a geologist, for goodness sake, purely because I had a fun-loving teacher, and subsequently got extremely good marks in geology.

I have a friend who as a kid used to practise with another boy. Basically they'd pitch balls back and forth to each other. Nothing more sophisticated than that – but they could do it for hours on end. It's a big ask to get a child to just pitch balls for hours, but a little game like that made all the difference. It's little wonder that he ended up playing off a three handicap.

Before I'd learnt the principles behind play practice, I

used to visit the sixth hole at Blackwood in the summer evenings after most of the golfers had left. I'd pitch and chip around the green and make up lots of little games to play. Not because I was being clever, but because the hard practice I used to do at the range was utterly exhausting and this at least allowed me to take a break while still practising.

I started out by trying to emulate Seve Ballesteros and his skill of using a three iron out of the bunker. It's not easy, but very possible – and it quite dramatically improves your confidence out of sand. My next game was to try and hit ten lob shots close to the hole with my eight iron. Then I'd attempt ten chip and runs with my lob wedge, or heat things up by hitting lobs off of very hard surfaces. In fact, I'd experiment with a host of little games that came to mind. It was great fun, but in an odd way it was also very hard practice. The next time I was out on the course, having to hit a high lob over a bunker from a good surface was suddenly incredibly easy compared to attempting the same thing with an eight iron or off packed mud.

So don't be afraid to give yourself a break and mess around a bit. Hard practice is just that – very hard. And ultimately this is a game that you should be hoping to have some fun with.

One last story to hammer this point home. When Phil Mickelson worked with Dave Pelz on some of the technical aspects of his putting or short game, they would have regular breaks. During these breaks Mickelson didn't, as you might have imagined in the past, nip off looking for cake. Nope – what Phil Mickelson, the greatest flop shot player in the world, did was play around and do flop shots. There's a wonderful video on YouTube of Phil hitting a shot over Dave Pelz's head as the two men stand almost nose-to-nose – a superb example of how play and hard practice mixed together can bear very juicy fruit!

50. Play the course on the range

A great way to enhance your practice time is to stand at the range and play the full course in your mind. All range practice should be about making sure you're not in a rarefied atmosphere where it is easy to just bash balls. That's why the hard practice is such a great idea – but as I've said earlier, hard practice is exhausting so sometimes you're looking for other ideas.

What I still do quite often at the range is play the full course in my mind during range sessions. Apart from the putting I'll attempt to play every shot on the course and vary my fairway shots depending upon how well I think my tee shot went.

To begin with I imagine I'm standing on the first tee, a par four at Blackwood. If I hit a great drive I can then imagine hitting a wedge into the green. But if that wedge is a little off then I'll have to imagine a little pitch to get me on and close to the flag. I'll take some small marker on the fairway as my imaginary pin position.

I then move to the second hole – a par five. I'll have to choose whether to use the driver or play it a little safer. And then I'll have to decide whether to go for the green on my second shot or lay up and see if my short game can get me close enough to birdie zone.

This little strategy helps tremendously both with making your range practice improve in terms of productivity but also in terms of teaching yourself how to think your way round the course and improve your general course management.

The 51st tip: Giving a little extra

When I first envisioned writing this book I always knew that I'd have a bit more than 50 tips to share, and thought I knew what that 'extra' tip was going to be. It would be based on a principle that I used during my golf practice whereby I'd always do a little more than I'd originally said I would. If I said I'd practice until 9.30 p.m. in the evening I'd make sure I slotted in an extra ten minutes. If I said I was going to hit 200 balls then I'd make sure to bring one extra bucket of twenty.

I was doing a couple of things with this process. Firstly I was attempting to teach myself some sporting discipline. I wanted to be able to make sure that, whether I ultimately succeeded or not, I could look myself in the mirror and know that I gave it my all, and maybe just a little bit more.

Secondly I knew that sometimes in those last ten minutes or twenty extra balls I quite often had little breakthroughs. For some reason they seemed to be very productive times. I'm not sure why but it worked, so it seemed like a good reason to keep them going.

But as a tip it slightly grates with me. It slightly reeks of 'look at me and how great I am' and that certainly isn't how I wanted to finish the book. So with that in mind I chose to keep one of the very best tips ever given to the end. It's also about as simple a tip as you'll ever hear.

It's another one from the wonderful Harvey Penick: 'Take dead aim.'

When I first read *Harvey Penick's Little Red Book* and saw this tip it looked almost *too* simple, but on my next round of golf I applied it as accurately as I could. I shifted from aiming vaguely down to a part of the fairway that I'd like to reach and focused in on a very specific mark. The resultant improvement in my accuracy was bewildering.

I'm sure you've heard it before but if you haven't, or are simply forgetting to apply it, make sure you 'take dead aim' on your next round of golf and see what a difference it makes.

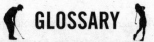

GLOSSARY

birdie – a score of one below par for a hole, e.g. completing a par three hole in two shots

bogey – a score of one shot over par for a hole, e.g. completing a par four hole in five shots

card a score – to submit a signed score card to a handicap committee or competition scorer. The card then counts towards your handicap.

cavity back iron – an iron with a largish head and a cavity or dent on the back of the face; a relatively 'easy to hit' style of iron

check spin – back spin on a wedge shot that makes the ball stop quickly

chip – a shot around the green that has a low trajectory of flight and that will run when it hits the ground

clubface – the part of the club that makes contact with the ball

drive – a shot taken with the driver; generally the longest shot a golfer can hit and the shot played when teeing off

driver head – the part of the driver that makes contact with the ball

eagle – a score of two below par for a hole, e.g. completing a par four hole in two shots

four-ball game – a group of four golfers all playing, generally over 18 holes. The cornerstone of friendly golf matches.

gimme – a short putt that (in friendly matches) you don't have to play because it's considered so easy that you couldn't miss it. Counts as one shot. Not allowed in competition play.

grooving – the process of practising a new change in your swing so that it becomes permanent

handicap – the numerical measure of a golfer's playing ability. This complicated system means that golfers can play matches on an equal footing regardless of ability. A golfer with a handicap of thirteen plays a round in an average of thirteen shots over par. Sometimes expressed as 'S/he plays off thirteen.'

hook – a shot that veers badly to the left (for a right-handed golfer)

hybrid club – a club that is relatively easy to hit and which can be used for a variety of situations, e.g. to chip with or replace a long iron. A recent invention.

iron – the clubs that are used most from the fairway (or tee) to hit the ball onto the green. Traditionally – before the development of hybrid clubs and wedges – this label covered all clubs between a one iron and a pitching wedge.

lie – the piece of grass that the ball lands on. A good lie will be easy to hit from, a bad lie will be difficult.

lipped putt – a putt that just catches the edge of the hole but fails to go in

mulligan – when you're playing with friends, and miss or fluff a shot, your playing partners can give you a mulligan, i.e. let you take the shot again without penalty and without counting the duff shot in your score. Only applies in friendly games of golf (never in competition) and only once per round (usually only on a drive).

par; level par – an estimated standard score for a hole or course that a good player should be able to make. A par three hole should be completed in three shots. A level par round is when a player goes round in a prescribed number of shots, e.g. going round a par-seventy-two course in seventy-two shots.

pitch – a shot around the green with a high trajectory which will generally stop quickly when it hits the ground

plug – a ball which is buried in the grass on a wet course, or in the sand in a bunker

putt – a shot played with the putter on the green

rib – a shot hit with the leading edge of the clubface; not a good shot

rough – the areas of vegetation and longer unkempt grass on a golf course

scratch golfer – a player who shoots an average of par; the equivalent of a handicap of zero

shag bag – a bag filled with practice balls

shank – a shot where the ball connects with the hosel (the part of the club where the club head meets the shaft) rather than the clubface and shoots off violently to the right; a truly horrible shot

slice – a very common shot among high handicappers; the ball starts relatively straight but quickly veers off to the right

spraying – randomly hitting shots to the left or right with no consistent direction

Stableford points system – a scoring system, commonly used in amateur competition, that allows golfers to receive points for each hole. These points are added up to make the final score, rather than the number of shots. It negates the effects of a couple of really bad holes because the player isn't penalised by being more than one over par.

thin – a ball struck by the leading edge of the clubface (generally not quite as bad as a rib)

top the ball – a terrible shot; the bottom of the club comes in contact with the ball and not the clubface

wedge: sand, lob, gap – a variety of clubs that help to get the ball close to the hole from different circumstances in and around the green

Acknowledgements

Following the publication of *Dream On*, a long list of people assisted me on my ongoing journey into the world of golf and I'm delighted to have made so many new friends, and found so many great colleagues, along the way.

The production of this book has created almost as much chaos around the house as *Dream On* did, so once again I need to acknowledge my lovely wife Lesley and beautiful daughter Aimee.

To the team at Digital Wildfire Golf, especially John Davy, Andrew Chooah, Daniel and David Batchelor, who help me keep the Break Par Blueprint members happy, and to those who have invested in the Break Par Blueprint, I offer my heartfelt thanks and respect.

I'd like to thank my agent Paul Feldstein and the various teams at Blackstaff Press, Skyhorse Publishing, MVG/Riva Verlag and The Best You, for investing time and money to help *Dream On* sell in multiple languages.

I'd like to thank Mark Pegg and Farren Blackburn for their tireless work in putting *Dream On* onto the big screen, and Richard Coyle for uncannily portraying my accent and mannerisms – in an irritatingly more appealing style.

Dream On had huge support from a number of key representatives of the press and in particular I'd like to thank Liam Kelly, Duncan Lennard, Stephen Watson, Dave Tindall, Matt Cooper, Chris Jones, Ron Kaspriske, John Shortt and the teams at *Today's Golfer* and *Golf Digest Ireland* who ran with the story long before I ever had a book to promote.

Beyond that, in no particular order, I'd like to thank Stuart Kennedy, Michael Donald, Jeremy Hinds, Stephen Roycroft, Paul and Karalyn Fields, Patrick Richardson, Professor Kathryn Saunders, my mastermind gang, Katriona and Richie Burrow, Karl Morris, Kathryn Thomson, Alan Thomson, James Rea, Rob Rea, Archie Rea, Andy Brown, Jim McLellan, Commander Kenneth Kenhalagin, Nick Jervis, Rob Ward, Patsy Allen, Peter and Rosemary Richardson.

And someone to keep your eyes on: Christian Johnson, a superstar in the making …

ALSO BY JOHN RICHARDSON

'I'm heartily recommending *Dream On* to anybody
who plays golf off any sort of handicap from ten upwards.'
John Inverdale, BBC Radio 5 Live

'DREAM ON'

One Hacker's Challenge to
Break Par in a Year

JOHN RICHARDSON

eBook

EPUB ISBN 978-0-85640-876-2

KINDLE ISBN 978-0-85640-877-9

Paperback

ISBN 978-0-85640-841-0

www.blackstaffpress.com
www.breakparblueprint.com
www.fiftygreatgolftips.com